THE MODERN DANCE

JOSÉ LIMÓN

ANNA SOKOLOW

ERICK HAWKINS

DONALD McKAYLE

ALWIN NIKOLAIS

PAULINE KONER

PAUL TAYLOR

THE
MODERN
DANCE

Seven Statements of Belief

EDITED AND WITH AN INTRODUCTION BY *Selma Jeanne Cohen*

Wesleyan University Press, Middletown, Connecticut

ISBN: *0–8195–6003–0*

Library of Congress Catalog Card Number: 66–14663

Manufactured in the United States of America

First paperback edition, 1969; fourth printing, 1977

Contents

Introduction: THE CATERPILLAR'S QUESTION   3

José Limón: AN AMERICAN ACCENT   17

Anna Sokolow: THE REBEL AND THE BOURGEOIS   29

Erick Hawkins: PURE POETRY   39

Donald McKayle: THE ACT OF THEATRE   53

Alwin Nikolais: NO MAN FROM MARS   63

Pauline Koner: INTRINSIC DANCE   77

Paul Taylor: DOWN WITH CHOREOGRAPHY   91

CONTRIBUTORS   104

Illustrations

José Limón   16

José Limón: rehearsing Sally Stackhouse, Louis Falco   19

The Emperor Jones: Lucas Hoving, José Limón   22

Missa Brevis: choreography, José Limón   25

Anna Sokolow: at rehearsal   28

The Question: choreography, Anna Sokolow: American Dance Theatre   31

Odes: choreography, Anna Sokolow: American Dance Theatre   32

Opus '65: choreography, Anna Sokolow: Robert Joffrey Ballet   34

Erick Hawkins   38

"Love Shouts Itself Transparent," from *Here and Now with Watchers:* Erick Hawkins, Nancy Meehan   42

Here and Now with Watchers: Erick Hawkins   46

Donald McKayle   52

Games: choreography, Donald McKayle   56

District Storyville: choreography, Donald McKayle: Carmen de Lavallade and ensemble   58

Alwin Nikolais   62

Imago: choreography, Alwin Nikolais   68

Vaudeville of the Elements: choreography, Alwin Nikolais   70

Allegory: choreography, Alwin Nikolais   72

Pauline Koner: in rehearsal   76

Pauline Koner   80

Pauline Koner: in performance   84

Paul Taylor   90

Tracer: Paul Taylor, Bettie de Jong   94

Insects and Heroes: Paul Taylor Dance Company   98

THE MODERN DANCE

Introduction:

THE CATERPILLAR'S QUESTION

WHEN I asked these choreographers to write about the modern dance, I anticipated the possibility of their feeling somewhat as Alice did when the Caterpillar took the hookah out of its mouth and addressed her in a languid, sleepy voice, saying: "Who are *you*?" To which Alice replied: "I — I hardly know, Sir, just at present — at least I know who I *was* when I got up this morning, but I think I must have changed several times since then."

In the lifetimes of these artists, the modern dance has changed. All of them have been instrumental in bringing about the changes, and all of them have changed themselves — some radically — from what they were when their careers began. The modern dance was once a fairly homogeneous entity. Not that all its exponents were alike — in fact, they gloried in their diversity — but they quite obviously shared many principles of belief. Today, the situation is far less clear. The ranks are not only diversified, but divided within themselves. So the modern dance has been several things in the course of time, and seems to be several more things right now. After a bit of thought, I began to wonder if all these various manifestations should — or even could — be brought together under a single name. However, the term is used, and perhaps I should at least attempt to find a thread of unity among its many, and apparently conflicting, uses.

In the course of compiling this book, I deliberately refrained from asking any of the choreographers to define the modern dance. Why make them uncomfortably self-conscious? As I had hoped, however, the definitions cropped up, quite naturally, in the course of their discussions. Also, as I had expected, they were all different.

3

What each did, of course, was define what the modern dance meant to him. At this point, the temptation was to say: "Well, good. The modern dance, then, is whatever it is, and all that it is, to its various exponents. A many-splendored thing. And let's let it go at that." That would have been easy. But basically unsatisfactory.

Then there was the choice of any number of previous definitions — all clear, pat, ready to be quoted. Yet no one of them seemed to cover the present situation. Barefoot dance? No, sometimes they wear shoes. Expressive dance? No, some of these choreographers are vehemently anti-expression.

So then, another possibility: a definition so flexible as to include them all — easily, comfortably. "Freedom from traditional rules" came most quickly to mind. But freedom from what tradition? Is any non-balletic choreography modern dance? And the ignorant are free. Does that make them modern? Apparently, none of these solutions would be of much practical value.

The only chance of finding an answer seemed to be the one implied by Alice, who admitted that she knew what she had been. By recalling what the modern dance had been when it started and by tracing it through its various evolutions, we may get a perspective on what it is today. If not a complete definition, at least a perspective . . .

In 1933, John Martin (who was then, and would be for many years to come, the dance critic of *The New York Times*) stated that the modern dance was a point of view. It was movement devised not for spectacular display, as was the ballet; not for self-expression, as was the interpretive dance current at that time; but it was movement made "to externalize personal, authentic experience." The ballet aesthetic, he contended, was concerned with visual beauty rather than emotion; when the ballet did deal with emotion, it did so in a manner so remote, so abstracted from realistic feeling that its creators in no way expected, or even desired, the audience to respond to its emotional content. The interpretive dance, while it dealt with experience, was unconcerned with its communication; the expression was an end in itself (therapeutic, we would call it today), which made it essentially untheatrical. The modern dance, on the other hand, externalized — projected, communicated — an emotion that was not only personal but "authentic." The choreographer felt the emotion deeply, but — further — was convinced that, by revealing his experience, he was also revealing a basic truth.

For America, the story had started at the turn of the century, when Isadora Duncan and Ruth St. Denis each began groping toward a style of dance that would allow a freedom of expression they could not find in the contemporary ballet. Both objected to the rigid formality and artificiality of the classic technique, to the superficiality of the themes it was using, to the triviality of its current aims. Duncan found the answer in natural movement, the unrestrained response to nature and to art as she felt the ancient Greeks had conceived it. Her dances were sometimes lyrical, sometimes heroic; always imbued with her vision of the Good and the Beautiful. St. Denis turned to the Orient, where the religious view of dance gave support to her concern with the spiritual values of the art. Later, with her husband Ted Shawn, she explored less exotic areas, but always with the aim of ennobling the concept of dance.

In the late twenties, however, the nature of the outlook was utterly changed when two renegades from Denishawn — Martha Graham and Doris Humphrey — rejected the sweetness-and-light approach of their predecessors. They created dance works with a toughness of fibre that had been bred — far from ancient Greece and the old Orient — by an age of skyscrapers, labor problems, and neuroses. Where the choreographers of the first years of the century had turned to past civilizations, aiming to revitalize the dance by infusing it with the enlightened aura of earlier cultures, those of the twenties stood rooted in the present. But it was a present colored by the ideas of *The Golden Bough,* by the writings of Freud and T. S. Eliot, by the paintings of Picasso and the music of Bartók. They too looked to the past, but to a more distant past — to the era of pre-history, to the time when man, uninhibited by arbitrary codes of mores, had expressed the full range of his primitive instincts. If the attack of Graham and Humphrey was more violent, it was because they had

5

more un-doing to accomplish. Both generations were concerned with externalizing personal, authentic experience. They differed radically, however, in their ideas of what kind of experience was important.

The second generation of the modern dance had to reject the idioms not only of classical ballet but also of Duncan and Denishawn. In none of their predecessors could they find a vehicle for the expression of contemporary ideas, and they asserted that dance could be a vehicle for the expression of such ideas. Doris Humphrey remarked then that the dancer should not be "concerned entirely with the graceful line and the fine, animal ease" that technical study provided; "he should also be concerned with his existence as a human being played upon by life, bursting with opinions and compulsions to express them." In principle, the ballet abstracted, idealized, the prowess and beauty of the body; not "played upon by life," but playing on life. That was fine — for the ballet. The heroism and nobility of Duncan and Denishawn were also very fine — for them. Now all this was seen as inadequate for an art that wanted to be significantly creative in the contemporary world.

Martha Graham wrote: "I do not want to be a tree, a flower, or a wave. In a dancer's body, we as audience must see ourselves; not the imitated behavior of everyday actions, not the phenomena of nature, not exotic creatures from another planet, but something of the miracle that is a human being, motivated, disciplined, concentrated."

The classical ballet could never have been accused of imitating everyday actions. As the ballet saw it, the miraculous aspect of the human being was its potential for dominion over the forces of nature — over its own weight, in the exultant leap; over gravity, in the joyously sustained balance; over its natural stiffness and awkwardness, in the high extension of the leg, effortlessly attained. To Denishawn, the exotic creature was the appealing character — the Egyptian or Hindu goddess, who shed about her the pure light of Truth. For Duncan, it was a simple process of taking what was best and most beautiful of the natural man.

The second generation found it impossible to settle for only the good. They acknowledged that there was love in man. Yes. But there were also hate and fear and jealousy. They spoke of all these with intensity and passion. The sweetness and light, they saw, were beautiful. But so were the depths of terror and hostility. Because they were true. And because they made man's achievement of love more difficult, more significant, more — miraculous.

The miracle was there; it had always been there; it was real. People had only forgotten. The manners and gentility of the Victorian age still cast their obscuring shadow over the emotions that were not mentioned in polite society. Now the modern dance choreographers felt the time had come to break through the veneer to reveal the terrible and wonderful beauty that lay beneath it. In Martha Graham's words, "to make apparent once again the inner hidden realities behind the accepted symbols."

They had to be extreme. They made their point by shock, though they did not set out to shock. They simply had to discard all the trappings of the familiar traditions to make their audience see with fresh eyes. By eliminating the decorative, the superficial, the glib polish, they aimed to dig down to the essence of significant movement; movement that had long been disguised by distortion and ornament; movement that — when laid bare — would be recognized as the symbol of long-hidden realities.

Martha Graham and Doris Humphrey started by looking for basic sources of movement, sources related to the primary instincts of the human animal. The ballet had used as its source the decorous positions of the dances of the courts of seventeenth-century European royalty. For Denishawn, it had been the stylization of the dances of Eastern temples. Duncan alone had apparently found a completely natural source; she traced all movement to the solar plexus. She herself had used this point instinctively, unerringly. From it she had derived movements of joy and grief, but there were other emotions she had not touched — guilt, anguish, remorse. These, apparently, were foreign to her nature, and she had no need to express them. The modern dance, however, needed them, and it needed a language of movement to embody them. So the 1920's started over — from the beginning.

7

For Martha Graham, it began with the act of breath — the start of life itself. Allowing the body to follow the natural ebb and flow of breathing, she watched what happened to the shape of the torso as it contracted in exhalation, expanded in inhalation. The next step was to intensify the dynamics of the act, taking the contraction as a sudden, spasmodic impulse, which could send the body into a fall, into a turn, into — as it evolved — any number of motions. It was a primitive use of energy — utterly new as an initiator of dance movement. Dramatically, it provided a basically natural but excitingly theatrical means of portraying the human being in terror, in agony, in ecstasy.

The approach of Doris Humphrey was equally basic, though totally different. Rather than turning to movement within the body, she viewed the body in relation to space. She saw movement as generated by effort to resist the pull of gravity — gravity as symbolic of all the forces that threaten man's balance, his security. She too discovered a principle of duality; for her it was the contrast of fall and recovery. Where Graham depicted the conflict of man within himself, Humphrey was concerned with the conflict of man with his environment. In both approaches, drama was inherent. But it was a kind of drama the public was unaccustomed to seeing. It was brutally honest; it was not pretty; it was not "nice."

Everything about the Graham and Humphrey productions was uncompromising. The time is now remembered as the "long woolens" period. No pretty costumes, just plain dresses of unadorned black jersey; no pink slippers, just bare feet; no elaborate scenery, just a functionally lighted cyclorama (of course the modern dancers could not have afforded fancy trimmings even if they had wanted them; their homes were the basements and attic walk-ups of Greenwich Village). The movements that derived from the primitive sources were as unornamented and unornamental as the costumes of the dancers. No graceful arms to enhance the visual picture; no brilliant technical feats. Instead of lyrical flow, there were sharply percussive thrusts. Instead of soaring with ease into the air, the dancers stamped on the bare floor with their bare feet. When they did jump, they jumped like creatures of the earth, fighting their way out of the mud. The hidden realities were apparent, all right. A lot of people didn't like them at all.

This made the life of the modern dance choreographers anything but easy. Boos and jeers are unpleasant to hear, and they have the further disadvantage of keeping potential ticket-buyers away from the box office. In time, however, largely through sheer persistence — though the persuasive powers of Mr. Martin in the pages of *The Times* helped a great deal — the public resistance gradually weakened. Not that the modern dance became popular; it has never been that. But it ceased to shock so much. Freud was no longer being ridiculed either. Gradually certain facts of art, as of life, were being at least recognized as inescapable realities.

At this point, the subsidence of hostility held great significance for the modern dance choreographers. It meant they no longer had to hammer at stubborn minds with reiterations of basic concepts. It meant they could explore, develop, apply those concepts to still further depths of experience. Great works had been created from the beginning. Now, after the initial period of struggle, the masterpieces began to flow.

There were ventures into primitive ritual, Americana, Greek myth, and social commentary. There were excursions into pure dance, with no overt dramatic content, that nevertheless achieved strikingly dramatic effects through rhythmic and spatial designs. There were adventures with structure — with stream-of-consciousness continuity, with dance punctuated by lines of spoken poetry, with the intricate weavings of allegory. Musical accompaniments ranged from silence, to Bach, to commissioned scores by experimental composers. Costume and décor were reinstated in fresh ways, with the use of simple but suggestive properties; nothing was there for purely decorative effect.

In time, the movement vocabulary itself was enormously expanded, becoming less relentless in its pounding earthiness, allowing softness — even tenderness — to emerge. For these too were part of man's essential nature. They had been submerged before only because the break with the past had had to be unmitigated in order to achieve the desired impact. Now, with the impact accomplished, the choreographers could safely broaden their palettes. Martha Graham and Doris Humphrey went from one revelation to another.

Yet the fever pitch of revolutionary fervor was passing. And with it was going that special sense of urgency, of combative aggressiveness, of excitement, that is engendered by revolutions. It was good to be rid of the jeering; the cheers were no less strong. Yet, without heated opposition, the triumphs were not quite so dazzling. As the masterpieces continued to appear, it was less necessary to fight in their defense. Though the revolution had been hard, it had been more stimulating.

To come to the modern dance in the course of this period of assimilation (as did all the writers in this book) has been, in some ways, more difficult than to enter the lists at the beginning. Faced with an idiom that was still new and working with choreographers who were still developing themselves, the novice was easily tempted to fall in line behind his elders. With the achievements of the leaders well in mind, the young choreographer had on the one hand a splendid precedent for innovation; on the other, a strong deterrent. It had been done; it did not need to be done again.

Besides, there were plenty of other problems to occupy the new generation. There were problems of refining the techniques, of making the dancers stronger and more versatile, of expanding theatricality and thematic range. There was plenty to do without trying to set out on a completely new road. It was really too soon anyway. The revolution was not that far away.

Looking back now, we can see that, actually, tremendous developments have taken place in the forty years since Graham and Humphrey broke the ties to Denishawn. The changes, however, occurred gradually; so they have seemed less drastic, less epoch-making in their repercussions. And there has been nothing so radical as the discovery of another new source of natural movement or of a completely different area of drama. Though the implications of the original concepts have been enormously extended, they have been extended within the framework of the thoughts of the founders. Remaining today are the ideas that initiated the American modern dance, but they are now applied in the context of a world that — while still dominated by the thinking of Freud — has now felt the impact of beatniks, astronauts, and the population explosion. To ignore these would be to reject the principles of the founders; they were vitally reality-oriented. Though some of the themes have altered and the technique has grown, the basic concept has not changed. The modern dance is still involved with the communication of personal, authentic experience.

However, this cannot be applied to all the choreographers now associated in the minds of the public with the modern dance; it cannot be applied even to all the choreographers represented in this volume. For the modern dance has not grown exclusively in the directions laid by its founders. Along the line of development, off-shoots have appeared, and their products are so different as to force us to question whether or not they really belong to the original shoot at all. Taller or shorter, Alice in Wonderland was still Alice — in the minds of her readers, at least, if not in her own. Yet this is simply not the case with the modern dance today. It has nothing to do with just the passage of time. Whether compared to the work of either the early or the late Graham or Humphrey, the new forms of choreography seem to have little, perhaps no, relation to what appears to be the main line of continuity in the modern dance.

What is so different? Well — just about everything. Gone are the movements derived from contraction and release, from fall and recovery, or from anything much resembling them. Gone, too, are the concern with terror and anguish and ecstasy. The new choreographers take their ideas from other sources — from chance juxtaposition, from serial music and action painting, from the current concepts of "happenings" and the theatre of the absurd. As for expressive purpose, they have none, save to say that the proper subject of dancing is dance. Why, they say, should we ask dancing to mean something beyond itself, which is so beautiful and exciting by itself? For the early modern dance, emotional motivation had been

11

essential; it was at once the cause and the aim of movement invention. With the new choreographers, emotional motivation has been deliberately eliminated from the scheme of composition, while other factors — chance, mathematics, musical or pictorial structure — have taken its place.

Even to an uninitiated public, the early modern dance was patently recognizable as an utterly personal and individual expression of deeply felt experience. The new choreographers counter everything about this. They are concerned with the movement rather than with the personality performing it, and they don't want the dance to express anything — especially feeling. The only experience in dance, they assert, should be the experience of the qualities of movement — fleet, spacious, soft, energetic, or whatever. But not emotion. That only takes the attention of the audience away from the essential thing, which is the kinetic image. Feeling is out; drama is out.

This had led the new choreographers to be accused of depersonalizing the dance, a verdict they answer in various ways: that it is impossible to depersonalize an art that uses the human body as its instrument; that they are seeking a transcendent form of identity; that it is depersonalized, but so what? Twenty years ago even the severest opponent of the modern dance would not have made such an accusation. If anything, he would have found the choreography embarrassingly personal.

Why did this new movement spring into being? The choreographers themselves assert that the modern dance was becoming so dramatic that it was turning into a kind of pantomime. The dance had lost sight of its true nature. Movement was no longer seen for its own beautiful sake; it was merely being used as a means to tell a story, and by such employment it was degraded. Their mission, therefore, is to bring the dance back to its true province by making it an end in itself. In this endeavor, they acknowledge the influence of trends toward abstraction, mechanization, and randomness in the other arts — this is the direction of our time, and after all they are modern. However, such concepts seem utterly remote from the original point of the modern dance. Can these new choreographers still be identified with the idiom of Duncan and Denishawn, of Graham and Humphrey?

Martha Graham had spoken of the function of dance in making apparent again the hidden realities behind the accepted symbols. To do this, an art must create new symbols, and in the beginning they are strange, uncomfortably unfamiliar — unacceptable. With time, however, the eye and the mind adjust to them; they become accepted. This is desirable, of course, since the point is to get the viewer to acknowledge the reality, the truth, behind the symbols. Yet, in the course of the process, the symbols lose their power. It is the shock that makes them work. They have to startle us into awareness, for it is only then that we are compelled to probe their meaning and discover what they have to tell us. The accepted symbol does not challenge us; we take it for granted.

When a symbol becomes accepted, an art may take either one of two courses in order to retain its vitality. The artist may keep the original symbol but develop and use it in fresh ways. Or he may discard it altogether, replacing it with a new one. Change the symbol he must, but he can do so either in degree or in kind. Which path he takes will depend on his view of reality: whether he agrees essentially with his predecessors but feels that areas of their vision remain to be explored; or whether he is convinced that the vision needs not simply extension but displacement. The modern dance choreographers of today are divided among themselves because some have chosen to explore, others to displace. Though the latter way is, to be sure, the more striking, the effect of the former is never so complacent as that of the reiteration of a comfortably familiar image. The modern dance choreographer is always concerned with the unacceptable symbol, the one that startles us into awareness. The pressure may be subtle or it may be obvious, but it is always there.

If the pressure is absent, the artist relinquishes his allegiance to the modern dance. If it shocks us into something less than awareness of realities — if the pressure is exerted only arbitrarily, to display ego or to attract the crowds — it does not belong to the modern dance. If, on the other hand, it permeates the creations of a so-called ballet choreographer (and the works of Antony Tudor, Jerome Robbins, and some of George Balanchine come immediately to mind), then those creations are modern. Theoretically, the ballet is opposed to the modern dance because it deliberately uses accepted symbols to depict an established ideology. When it ceases to do so, the categorical name becomes meaningless.

This has nothing to do with value judgments. A ballet is not bad because it employs accepted symbols; it merely serves a different function, and it may or may not serve that function well. A modern dance work may fail too. Many have. This does not invalidate the concept of function that identifies it. For it can be identified.

The modern dance is a point of view, an attitude toward the function of art in the contemporary world. As that world changes, the modern dance will change, for the symbols will again — as they become acceptable — lose their power to evoke the hidden realities. They will again have to be recharged, revitalized; even demolished and re-created anew in order to serve their function. Unless this happens, the modern dance is not modern — it is dead.

The modern dance is an art of iconoclasts.

EACH choreographer represented in this book was asked to divide his contribution into two parts. First, he was to set forth, generally, his ideas on the modern dance. Second, he was to describe what he would do if he were given a commission to create a dance under the most (unrealistically) favorable conditions — any number of dancers, any kind of music, costumes, etc. Also (most unrealistic) he was to assume that he had unlimited funds at his disposal. There was only one restriction: his dance had to deal with the theme of the Prodigal Son.

Here, then, are seven essays on the modern dance. And seven descriptions of dances on the theme of the Prodigal Son.

José Limón

AN AMERICAN ACCENT

I

THE ballet as an art is an old and established tradition, not the least of the many splendors of European civilization. One cannot fully savor the essence of European culture without recognizing the importance of the ballet, for nations make themselves known through their dances. We gain a more profound insight into the soul of Spain, of India, of Cambodia, Bali, China, Korea, and Japan from their dances than from any of their other arts.

Italy, the mother of the ballet; France, its nursemaid; and Imperial Russia, which saw it to its glittering maturity, reveal themselves to the world in every movement, gesture, and configuration of their prodigious creature. The great Medici were not only statesmen, rulers, and patrons of the arts; they were connoisseurs and lovers of the *ballo*. One of their daughters, the illustrious Catherine, transplanted it to the court of France, where — amidst the turmoil of a savage century — it grew and flourished, elegant and serene. Subsequently the *Roi Soleil* gave it the prestige of his august participation. The Italian immigrant was now as royal as the dynasty of the House of Bourbon, as French as Versailles, and henceforth its code of movement, its vocabulary, was to be expressed in the French tongue.

The Imperial Romanovs, in transforming Russia from an Asiatic despotism into a state with the outward trappings of a Western nation, took care that the ballet, that most Western of the arts, should certify and confirm the new status. So superbly did the ballet flourish in the climate of the Muscovite empire — favored by Imperial patronage and the astonishing aptitude of the Russian temperament

José Limón (photo: Jack Mitchell)

17

and physique — that before long it surpassed the product of the regions of its origins. The formidable Imperial Russian Ballet came to be to the nation what armies, scientific achievements, and ancient ruins were to other nations. The Russian Ballet became the envy and wonder of the Western world. It became not only an art but a *lingua franca* of urbanity and civilization.

Yet it is a curious property of human accomplishment that — when seemingly at its zenith — it contains the seeds of the dissolution that could destroy it. It was at this high noon of the popularity of the ballet that an American girl rose in the cultural firmament and incredibly seemed to eclipse its radiance. Isadora Duncan, a rebel, an iconoclast was — like all revolutionaries — bold and uncompromising in her attack. She declared that the ballet was decadent, effete, ugly, artificial; that its training and technique, its turned-out positions, its rigidities, its obsessive use of the pointes, were odious, distorted, and against all nature. It made the human entity into a mechanical puppet, moving jerkily from one affected pose to another to the accompaniment of execrable music. With peerless audacity, she flung out her accusations and defiance, not only in the capitals of the West but in that holy of holies of the ballet itself — St. Petersburg.

It is dangerous for an art, however "classical," to become so rigid, so fossilized, as to lose the freshness, resiliency, and vigor of its original impulse. The art of the ballet during this era, in Western Europe and especially in Russia, seems to have fallen into such a state as to justify the ardent accusations of Isadora Duncan. Where the Parisians, with their cynical predilection for *joie de vivre,* made of their ballet a toy — a *petit rien,* a bagatelle — the Russians, with a heavy, despotic hand, transformed it into an instrument of the Imperial order — as were the church, the apparatus of government, and the armed forces. And they made it, like these, impervious to new ideas and to change.

Duncan — a scandal, a danger, and a delight — split the artistic world in half. There were those who saw her as a crude amateur, a shameless exhibitionist with no technique; there were those who

José Limón: rehearsing Sally Stackhouse, Louis Falco

sensed in her a challenge, a revelation, and a portent for the future of the dance. It was fortunate for this future that artists of the caliber of Michel Fokine accepted the disturbing challenge to stagnation. So came into being, away from Czarist authority, in the freer ambient of the West, the glories of the Ballets Russes.

It has been said that the modern dance is a temporary phase — that it has not sent down roots like the ballet and cannot, like it, endure. Yet the modern dance began with Duncan shortly after 1900. Now, in 1966, one would have to be myopic not to see that it is far from finished. An art that has produced such figures as Ruth St. Denis, Ted Shawn, Martha Graham, Doris Humphrey, Charles Weidman, Helen Tamiris, Hanya Holm, Pauline Koner, Anna Sokolow, Alwin Nikolais, Sophie Maslow, Pearl Lang, and Merce Cunningham, and can look to the vigor of a new generation, has a more than fair prospect of enduring. Especially when its principles exist and flourish, not only in its own milieu but in the works of the leading ballet companies. Let us make no mistake about it: if by "modern dance" one means a state of mind, a cognizance of the necessity of the art of the dance to come to terms with our time, then that art cannot be relegated to the position of a merely transitory influence. The modern dance is here to stay, whether it is performed barefoot or *sur les pointes*.

Modern dance is not a "popular art." It is not suitable, as is the traditional ballet, to advertise automobiles, vacuum cleaners, rugs, or hair dyes in newspapers or magazines or on television. A pretty ballerina in a pert tutu and pink toe shoes is a much more fetching sales pitch than a vision of a barefoot dancer in a species of ecstasy or suffering. On the other hand, talented — or sometimes merely clever — choreographers have taken the modern dance and adapted it to serve very successfully in musical shows, television, and films, in much the same manner that adaptations of Debussy, Bartók, and Schönberg have found their way into popular songs and the sound tracks of films from Hollywood. The use of serious art in any of its forms for less than its exalted purpose may be open to question. The fact remains that the multitudes who flock to musicals and movies would have had no contact with the contemporary arts (however diluted their presentation in commercial form) if they had not encountered them in this way.

I discovered, however, early in my career, after I had appeared in Broadway shows as both a dancer and a choreographer, that the commercial form and the serious form of the modern dance were incompatible. One had to devote one's self exclusively to one or the other. They could not mix. The serious dance demands an incorruptibility that makes no concessions to so-called popular taste. This has resulted in a dance that not only is not popular, it is not fashionable — it is not chic.

Yet it is a reality and a necessity of our time. Not every artist is disposed toward the Academy, great as it is in tradition and accomplishment. An American idiom is needed to say what cannot be said within the vocabulary of the European dance. This idiom, created by generations of American artists, is in essence non-academic; in principle, experimental; in practice, eclectic and inclusive.

Doris Humphrey declared that, as a young dancer, she was trained to perform — besides the traditional ballet — Spanish, Hindu, Siamese, Balinese, Japanese, Chinese, and other exotic dances. The time came, however, when she became aware that she had no identity as an American, and that all her dancing was — in effect — an impersonation, a masquerade. It was always something borrowed from Europe or the Orient. She could very well have accepted this, as so many young artists did and still do. But she suffered a deep discontent, knowing that for her this was not the way. What to do? What was there to look to as an American dance? Square dances? The American Indian? Negro jazz? Tap dancing? None of these offered a solution. Even the great Duncan, in rejecting the ballet, had reverted to the Hellenistic era. Doris Humphrey saw that the dance idiom she sought would have to be invented. Its creation would be a hard and long voyage of discovery into the inner self; its origins, its awareness and experience and capacity as an American self living

21

in the twentieth century. This dance would spring from the temper of her time.

I was fortunate in coming as a novice to her studio at the precise moment when, in company with Charles Weidman, she had embarked on this voyage of discovery. My experience with the dance had been, in a sense, similar to hers, though — by comparison — miniscule. As a child in Mexico, I had been fascinated — as any child would be — by Spanish jotas, Mexican jarabes, and Indian bailes. Later, across the border, I had seen tap dancers and ballet dancers. All this seemed interesting enough to watch, but to me it was something for girls to do. It never occurred to me as something a man would be caught dead doing. Then pure accident brought me to a performance by Harald Kreutzberg. What I saw simply and irrevocably changed my life. I saw the dance as a vision of ineffable power. A man could, with dignity and a towering majesty, dance. Not mince, prance, cavort, do "fancy dancing" or "show-off" steps. No: dance as Michelangelo's visions dance and as the music of Bach dances.

Kreutzberg had given me the illumination to see the road. But he was a German; his visions were Gothic. They became him; but I was by origin a Mexican, reared in the United States. I must find the dance to say what I had to say about what I was. In Doris Humphrey I found a master who knew that every dancer, being an individual, was an instrument unique and distinct from any other, and that in consequence this dancer must ultimately find his own dance, as she had found hers. I was instructed, stimulated, trained, criticized, encouraged to look for and find my own dance. I was not to ape my teachers. Early, I was encouraged to compose dances. I was admonished: "You will compose one hundred bad dances before you compose one good one."

I view myself as a disciple and follower of Isadora Duncan and of the American impetus as exemplified by Doris Humphrey and Martha Graham, and by their vision of the dance as an art capable of the sublimity of tragedy and the Dionysian ecstasies. I try to compose works that are involved with man's basic tragedy and the grandeur of his spirit. I want to dig beneath empty formalisms, displays of

23

The Emperor Jones: Lucas Hoving, José Limón

technical virtuosity, and the slick surface; to probe the human entity for the powerful, often crude beauty of the gesture that speaks of man's humanity. I reach for demons, saints, martyrs, apostates, fools, and other impassioned visions. I go for inspiration and instruction to the artists who reveal the passion of man to me, who exemplify supreme artistic discipline and impeccable form: to Bach, Michelangelo, Shakespeare, Goya, Schönberg, Picasso, Orozco.

With the years, I have become blind to the blandishments and seductions of the romantics. I am impatient with the sounds of the Schumanns, the Mendelssohns, the Gounods, and the Massenets. The literature of the romantics, their architecture, and their fashions arouse in me a feeling of aversion. The undisciplined and sometimes fatuous exhibition of the romantic soul in exquisite torment — whether in music, painting, or dance — leaves me cold. This saccharine and maudlin view of the human condition is to me specious and decayed. I am happy that the Cézannes, the Debussys, the Duncans, the Ibsens, the Dreisers, and the O'Neills have given us back a more adult view of our humanity.

I deplore the artist who makes of his art a withdrawal from the travail of his time; who sterilizes and dehumanizes it into empty formalism; who renounces the vision of man as perfectable, a "golden impossibility," and makes him into the shabby scarecrow of the beatniks; who forgets that the artist's function is perpetually to be the voice and conscience of his time. It was Doris Humphrey who first taught me that man is the fittest subject for choreography. And Martha Graham continues triumphantly to prove that his passions, grandeurs, and vices are the ingredients of great dance, great theatre, and great art.

It is important to preserve the traditional. It is part of our heritage, and as such it is to be cherished. But the modern idioms should be left to the individual to be kept resilient, venturesome, experimental, unhampered. The individual contribution is what gave us cultural maturity and independence from Europe in all our arts. Were it not for this, dancers in America would have remained docile

Missa Brevis: choreography, José Limón

provincials, creating nothing original. By learning to speak in an American idiom, they have enriched the world.

II

The tie between father and son is one of the most baffling of human relationships. Every man looks for his son, hoping through him to achieve his immortality. Every son rejects the father, and every father suffers for this, yet remains ultimately loving and compassionate. The wound that the son inflicts comes as a kind of blessing, a benediction. I feel poignantly the wisdom and beauty of this parable.

In composing dances, I tend to turn to my own experience. Therefore, as I did in *The Traitor,* I would set this version of the Prodigal Son in the present time. I would try to find in it something cogent and pertinent to our time. *The Traitor* was the result of my horror at the execution of two Americans, husband and wife, in peacetime, for treason and espionage against their country; and the spectacle of Russians who, in turn, abandoned their country and defected to the West.

I have been a son, and I have known the adolescent's antagonism toward his father, that instinctive hostility and resentment of his authority. I rebelled, resolving to be the exact opposite of my father. Years later — too late — I realized that I had been wrong and had misjudged him completely. Then I discovered that he had always understood and had been forgiving.

My dance, therefore, would have only two characters, a protagonist and an antagonist, eternally opposed and irreconcilable. They would represent the conflict between authority and the rebel, orthodoxy and the heretic, order and chaos. The dancers would perform on an austere, bare stage, hung with black velour, superbly lit throughout the action. There would be, for the son, no adventures, festivities, or orgies during his flight from his father's house. In this case, such scenes would be obvious and superfluous. I would show the son's defection from the virtues of his father's love as a subjective analysis of my own rebellious excesses, typical of all youth, and I would show them in an evocative solo of some substance. I would then examine the father's reaction in a dance symbolic of the desolation of those rejected and abandoned. Compassion is a bitter thing, for it leaves the compassionate without the solace that hatred and contempt bring. They must endure with their understanding and their pity.

I would not show the return of the chastened Prodigal in a sentimental dénouement with a fatted calf. There would be no touching filial repentance, no tender paternal acceptance. For the son can never return to the paternal bosom; he can only come back and continue to face the adversary anew. So I would have only a confrontation with new eyes and a new awareness. It would be austerely restrained and unemotional. Ultimate repentance and ultimate forgiveness are serene beyond sentiment. They are resolved in utter and private loneliness, for each man — forgiving father and errant son — must fail to reach or know the other. Each can regard the other only across a dark gulf, a chasm. In this scene, the abyss would deepen and intensify as the two dancers, remote as two planets, would circle — ostensibly for an eternity — each in his own lonely orbit. This I have found is my experience, and this is how I would — and probably will — compose a dance on the theme of the Prodigal Son.

I would persist in my emulation of the artists whom I revere. I would work to the limit of my capacity to utilize the elements of this theme with the utmost passion, with complete formality, with all simplicity.

Anna Sokolow: at rehearsal (photo: Herbert Migdoll)

Anna Sokolow

THE REBEL AND THE BOURGEOIS

I

I hate academies. I hate fixed ideas of what a thing should be, of how it should be done. I don't like imposing rules, because the person, the artist, must do what he feels is right, what he — as an individual — feels he must do. If we establish an academy, there can be no future for the modern dance. An art should be constantly changing; it cannot have fixed rules.

The trouble with the modern dance now is that it is trying to be respectable. The founders of the modern dance were rebels; their followers are bourgeois. The younger generation is too anxious to please, too eager to be accepted. For art, this is death. To young dancers, I want to say: "Do what you feel you are, not what you think you ought to be. Go ahead and be a bastard. Then you can be an artist."

The modern dance should be non-conformist. We should not try to create a tradition. The ballet has done that, and that's fine — for the ballet. But not for us. Our strength lies in our lack of tradition. Some say that the big change came in the late 1920's, and now is the time for the modern dance to assimilate and solidify. That's all wrong, because it is like building on still another tradition. Without change there can be no growth, and not enough change is going on today.

My quarrel with this generation is that they copy their teachers, and it's their own fault. They don't want freedom; they want to be told what to do. Why don't they realize they don't have to believe everything teacher says? They ought to disagree; they ought to argue.

29

Of course it's not all the fault of the student. Too often, teachers are merely polite when they should be provocative. They ought to shock. Look at Louis Horst. At eighty, he was still fresh and bold. The good teacher does not teach rules; he stimulates. He shows the students what he knows and inspires them — to go and do something else.

Learning rules cannot produce an artist. What is an artist? What is the nature of the creative process? These are things we can't know; they can't be explained. The creative teacher opens doors for his students to see what life is, what they are. They have to take it from there.

It is easier and quicker to teach by rule, but in the end it's no good. To learn to choreograph, you just have to mess through it for a while. Most people feel they have to "fix" a dance, they have to make it "neat." No — it's better to have disordered life, but to have life. The modern dance is an individual quest for an individual expression of life.

The new generation have not really faced themselves; they don't know what it is they want to say. Most of their choreography is vague. It doesn't come organically from the person. It can't, because the choreographer doesn't know who he is or how he feels. So he tries to cover up his confusion by giving his dances fancy titles, by being intellectual. Dance is not intellectual. It deals with deep emotion.

Choreography always reflects the character of the creator. We see in the person's work what he asks from life and from art. Some want only to be entertained, so they offer us only entertainment. Others see life as a tremendous, mysterious force, and this is reflected in their work. Of course there are times when we want to be entertained. Life is not all deep emotion. Art should recognize all our needs.

I don't believe in ivory towers. The artist should belong to his society, yet without feeling that he has to conform to it. He must feel that there is a place for him in society, a place for what he is. He must see life fully, and then say what he feels about it. Then, although

30

The Question: choreography, Anna Sokolow: American Dance Theatre (photo: Herbert Migdoll)

he belongs to his society, he can change it, presenting it with fresh feelings, fresh ideas.

The important thing is that the art being created now be related to now, to our time. The artist must be influenced by his time, conditioned by the life around him. If he is not, his viewpoint is limited by the past, and turns back instead of going forward. If he draws on the ever-changing life around him, his work will always be fresh and new. Art should be a reflection and a comment on contemporary life.

Yet some people are afraid to use life, feeling that art should be something apart, something isolated from reality. I once had a student in Israel who had been in a German concentration camp. You would never have known it from the windblown *schöene tänze* that she composed for me. They amounted to — nothing. I asked her: "Why don't you use your experience?" Then she created a marvelously powerful study based on the reality she had known.

Anyone, however, can have a good idea for a dance. In itself, that's not enough. There must be form as well as concept; both matter — what you feel and how you express it. First, the choreographer sees his idea in terms of movement, as the painter see his in terms of color, line, and mass. This happens spontaneously. Movements are not intellectually contrived but are evoked by emotional images. The only intellectual process is the one that puts these spontaneously conceived movements together into a form that works as a whole.

A sense of form, a feeling for construction, can be learned. But there are no rules. How, then? Well, you look at forms, at structures around you. Look at the shape of a box or a bottle; look at the lines of a table. It is easier to see form in life today than it was in the era of the Baroque, when forms were all covered with ornamentation. I don't like elaborated design. I like naked structure. In the theatre, I am anti-décor and anti-costume.

Progress in art comes through the quest for new forms. The artists I most admire are the ones who have dared to break with traditional forms — artists such as Joyce and Picasso and Balanchine. Pure form is not cold, because it is an abstraction from reality; its

33

Odes: choreography, Anna Sokolow: American Dance Theatre (photo: Herbert Migdoll)

source is life itself. Form for form's sake is dull, contrived, intellectual. True form comes from reducing reality to its essential shape, as Cézanne did with the apple. In the hands of an artist, form is emotional, exciting. You feel that there is a reason for everything being there, just as it is. There is nothing superfluous, because the artist has stripped his work down to the bare essentials. And an audience responds emotionally to this purity, this inevitability of form, which is beauty.

It takes courage to be so simple. I dig Balanchine because he is daring in his simplicity. Look at the last movement of *Ivesiana* — the dancers just walk on their knees. This is bold; it's modern. It's ballet, but it's modern.

I think there will always be a basic, technical distinction between modern dance and ballet, because the modern conception of training is different. But in dance works there should be no idioms. It's not technique that makes a dance modern; you can have a modern dance on pointes. It's not subject matter, either. Tudor's *Pillar of Fire* has a romantic story like *Giselle,* but it doesn't reflect the conventional concept of romance. It's a difference in point of view. The modern attitude does not eliminate fantasy or romantic and poetic ideas. But we don't handle them the way the nineteenth century did. We are not representational; we are imaginative.

I have never told stories in dance, though I have always been strongly dramatic. I never plan a dance. I do it, look at it, and then say: "Yes, I see what I am trying to do."

For me, *Lyric Suite* was a turning point. It was then that I began to find a language of movement for myself. I see no reason to fight a personal language; it's an organic statement of the person. But one must not rest on it. The important thing is to stretch the personal vocabulary so that it does not remain static. This does not mean changing its essential nature. One can remain one's self without repeating a statement.

When I first heard the *Lyric Suite,* I was fascinated with Berg's music, because I could see nothing lyric about it. Then it began to evoke dance images for me. After it was done, I saw the first move-

35

Opus '65: choreography, Anna Sokolow: Robert Joffrey Ballet (photo: Herbert Migdoll)

ment as an expression of man; the second, as the quality of woman.

Rooms was choreographed without music. I wanted to do something about people in a big city. The theme of loneliness and non-communication evolved as I worked. I like to look into windows, to catch glimpses of unfinished lives. Then I ask: "What is there, and why?" Then I thought of using chairs as if they were rooms, each dancer on his own chair, in his own room, isolated from all the others though physically so close to them.

Jazz was the right music for *Rooms.* I have always been interested in jazz; I find it one of the greatest and most profound expressions of our times. It makes me think. In *Rooms,* jazz was used for the dramatic and psychological depiction of individuals. In *Opus 58* I used jazz for an over-all aura of the sounds and rhythms of today. I wanted the feeling of a new era, one where life is violent and precarious, and the individual seems unimportant.

Then came *Dreams,* which was my indictment of Nazi Germany. When I started, I had only the idea of dreams, but they became nightmares, and then I saw they were related to the concentration camps. Once this had happened, I intensified the theme by focusing on it.

In *Opus 63* I just started out to do something in unison movement. But the work talked back to me. After a wild Bossa Nova, with everyone going at each other, I ended it with the dancers just walking. It had a quality of strength, like religion; a belief that the spiritual thing will survive. But my works never have real endings; they just stop and fade out, because I don't believe there is any final solution to the problems of today. All I can do is provoke the audience into an awareness of them.

II

I have always been interested in the Bible and curious to see how I might arrive at a movement style that has a Biblical feeling. The Imbal company has achieved this in its way; I must find my own way. There is the influence of the landscape, of dryness and heat. There is the quality of a desert people. There is the feeling of the culture of the Middle East, a mixture of the Greek and the Oriental.

There is the Bible itself, which deals with big and eternal emotions. We are always tempted; we always sin, because we are human. There is nothing sentimental about the Bible. It is not bound by all those horrible, Victorian concepts of good manners and little, blown-up feelings, with everyone going around being "nice" and thinking that only minority groups have passions. The Bible has tremendous force and vitality. It is really modern.

So in my telling of *The Prodigal Son,* I would try to capture the qualities of the Bible. I think I would do it in modern dress. I would use music of today — probably the jazz of Teo Macero — but asking him to work in the qualities of such ancient instruments as the drum, harp, and flute. I might use words as well as movement — possibly poetry.

Anna Sokolow
THE REBEL AND
THE BOURGEOIS

Erick Hawkins

PURE POETRY

I

THE first time I saw pictures of Isadora Duncan, I simply fell in love with her with all the ardent tenderness that a young man of seventeen brings to such a love. Later on I saw pictures of Shanta Rao and fell in love again, and later still, when I saw her on stage — with her irresistible, sensuous female radiance — I fell even more in love with all the passion that a grown man can bring to something he knows is a treasure. Whatever discoveries I have since made in perception or attention or the pure fact of movement I owe to these loves. Whenever I have the good fortune to find another tender gesture for some new dance, I owe it to them. They taught me that the important essence of all dancing is *movement quality*, and its excellence or lack of excellence. I quickly discovered that the wondrous, immediate knowledge of existence that you get in the pure fact of movement can come only if you find that inner quality. I soon realized that pure movement is decorative, instead of significant, if the inner quality is lacking.

Ballet did not satisfy me because it was too much like a diagram and, for me, too much of the indescribable pure poetry of movement had to be left out. It moved like a diagram because it had developed at a period in Western culture that emphasized theoretical knowledge and — if not puritanical — at least extremely unsensuous attitudes toward the body.

When Jacques Barzun speaks of "the treason of the artist," he speaks of the wonderful breakthrough of modern art at the turn of the century to an undiagrammatic way of thinking. Then, with the

39

current pressure of technology and one kind of scientific thought, the backtracking, or "treason," of the contemporary artist turned against this vision toward a kind of pseudo-scientific art, or really a science-fiction.

Today we are losing the poetry of art, and this poetry can never be conceptual or diagrammatic. It must preserve that initial innocence of the sensuous. We now have a taste for the overblown, the complex, the unsensuous, and the anonymous. When the composer Lucia Dlugoszewski shakes one of her delicate paper rattles, I know she has the chance of being more poetic than a whole symphony orchestra.

We have to recognize that we live in a transcending culture. Non-Western peoples, who have a traditional culture, merely keep rediscovering their unchanging, unhistorical intuition of excellence and the good life. But once science comes into the picture, we have history and a constantly changing attitude toward what is the good life, and this we call a transcending culture. It constantly demands a constantly changing justification for the arts. Since ballet and modern dance are both part of a transcending culture, they are both temporary, both on trial, until they prove and re-prove their excellence and their potential for the good life.

Modern dance came into existence because it had to. It came into existence in recognition of some obvious facts: namely, that the codification of movement, technique, and aesthetics called "ballet" was only a part of the way Westerners, including and especially Americans, could dance; that as the ideas of the good life altered with time, so the ideas of how dance could be danced altered; that as the philosophical ideas of the other arts were changing, so those of dance would change.

The turning point that led to the manifestation called "modern dance" came when Isadora Duncan had a new idea of the human being — specifically the human being in this specific place America, stemming in a direct line from Melville, Thoreau, Emerson, and Whitman, and going back for confirmation to the idea of the human being as stated in the classical period of Greece — the only place in all of Western history where the human body was considered beautiful, a worthy and loved and equal partner with the "soul-mind"; where the human body, male or female, was not distorted by costume, conduct, and pinched puritanical and partial concepts of the human body-soul. Only when the body was re-recognized and freed could a new art of dance arise in the West.

Then Ruth St. Denis and later Ted Shawn, in their search for antecedents, for some connection with a sensuous past that could accept dancing, went afield for confirmation of their intuition to the non-Western peoples, to the Orient. The intuitions of these three were glorious and are still to be built upon. All three were bright enough to see how much more was possible in dance movement than traditional ballet offered. They saw that, for all the virtues of its technique, it was partial in scope.

Isadora Duncan was the first dancer in the West to intuit a kinesiological truth: that human movement starts in the spine and pelvis, not in the extremities — the legs and arms. That is: human movement, when it obeys the nature of its functioning, when it is not distorted by erroneous concepts of the mind, starts in the body's center of gravity and then — in correct sequence — flows into the extremities.

Photographs and drawings of Isadora Duncan indicate — and her writings try to say this too — that she conceived the essence of movement to lie in transition, not in position. When she says "Study Nature," she means "flow organically," in arcs, like the spring of a cat, the wiggle of a water moccasin, the gallop of a horse, the wave on a beach, the toss of a ball, the bellying of a sail — not like a man's mind-contrived, inorganic machine, which essentially cannot move but only take positions.

It is significant that the official symbol of the School of American Ballet is Leonardo da Vinci's drawing of a man's body as it is arranged diagrammatically, geometrically, ready for scientific measurement and for scientific (rather than felt) relationships. The change to a fresher and more comprehensive principle is what makes modern dance.

41

"Love Shouts Itself Transparent," from *Here and Now with Watchers:* Erick Hawkins, Nancy Meehan

Ballet denies the sensuous body in technique, costume, and subject matter. The image of the woman on toe is the limited, erotic image, which was permitted men with all the baggage of erotic fears that characterized Western culture from the Middle Ages until the revolution of Freud. In its subject matter, the early modern dance merely expressed these fears; the fearless and radiant sensuality of Shanta Rao is still a thing for us to have the courage to learn.

On the cover of *Newsweek* in the spring of 1964, George Balanchine was photographed with a number of women dancers. The caption below was: "Ballet Is Woman." This was correctly stated. Ballet is geared for the woman dancer on toe. In 1903 Isadora Duncan saw that this was a false artistic and kinesthetic premise, and that we had better join the rest of the world, which does its dancing with the sensitivity of the beautiful, naked, undistorted, and felt human foot.

The emphasis on the technique of the toe shoe in ballet leaves the male dancer as a supernumerary (a little like the guy who carries a spear in *Aida*). But the wiser all races become, the more they find a beautiful, complementary equality between man and woman. Whether you read Erich Fromm or Edward Albee, it is clear that if we do not solve the conflict between men and women, our culture will destroy itself. One of the challenges of our moment in history is to find the true and beautiful meeting between men and women, and when dance uses the human body as its material, it of all the arts is required to meet the challenge most vividly. It cannot today afford a technique that jeopardizes this vision.

The modern dance has had two goals. One was to develop a larger and more comprehensive total technique with which to train the body so that it could fulfill the vision of a new beauty of human movement in the Western world. The other was to use this completely trained instrument to convey a more far-ranging subject matter in the art.

Before she returned to India after her last performance here in 1964, Shanta Rao remarked to me that while she had not seen much modern dance in America, she wondered from what she had seen

43

why it was so full of "frustration." Frustration is certainly a mighty frail area of human experience on which to build a blossoming art. The challenge of a new modern dance is to take the responsibility of maturity.

Many fine, mature works of art were made in modern dance between 1931 and 1964, but there has always been an unhealthy aspect as well. This has stemmed from the work of certain dance artists who, like those in other fields, considered it appropriate to portray anxiety and neurosis, and to report our state of confusion. My opinion, however, is that the Western dance artist is ready to learn from the Oriental that his function is to present ideas of enlightenment, and in this way to reconfirm the intuitions that each member of the audience has latent within him about how he can mature and fulfill all the possibilities of a complete and meaningful life. I suspect that the neurotic quality, the wallowing in confusion of much of serious art in our time, is what has alienated the broad mass of people who gravitate toward "entertainment" rather than immature, self-expressive, unhealthy art.

Shanta Rao's objection to modern dance subject matter can be seen from the beginning of formal Western thought on aesthetics. The pros and cons of Plato's discussion of art in *The Republic* have cropped up ever since his time. But his reasoning is incontrovertible and is parallel to traditional Oriental aesthetics. Plato says if you desire the ideal of maturity in all human beings, you will show in your arts only models of maturity and will not wallow in "reporting" strife, inadequate ways of how men and women get along together. You will not titillate people with patterns of immature behavior and paltry, vulgar images of the self, and then say: "Life is like this; what a mess!" You will not end only in unresolved discouragement, negativism, and Shanta Rao's "frustration." Modern artists try to justify this negative titillation by saying that they are not Pollyannas. Actually they are another kind of Pollyanna, hanging onto little, private neuroses, because without them they would feel naked and insignificant. The resulting art forms are melodrama. Let us stop fooling ourselves that these ever reach the truth of tragedy.

It is currently a popular idea to unify the modern dance achievements the way ballet is unified and to produce an impersonal company that could perform all modern dances. To unify the modern dance in a universal, non-egotistical technique is a commendable idea. It is right that as soon as possible the truth of how the body would be trained as a dancing instrument, without limitations and personal eccentricities, should be arrived at and used. This would stop the technical self-indulgence of many modern dancers and would set aside the unfortunate myths of idiosyncratic dancers, who have claimed for their personal limitations the label of a universal technique. There would then be finally no need for modern dancers to study ballet, because what was useful in the balletic training of a complete instrument would be assimilated into this larger point of view.

However, to jeopardize the glorious, unparalleled vitality in the diversity of modern dance choreography by arbitrarily fixing an impersonal dance company geared to perform all works would be to deny the glorious reason for its coming into existence in the first place. Everyone in Manhattan who is aesthetically alive groans to see another standard skyscraper go up — standard because it is cheaper. We must not forget that the true American dream is that exact, intense individualism and lack of conformity and passionate diversity. We are challenged in our moment of history not to lose this treasure that is our unique cultural heritage. We are lucky to be modern dancers. We have ahead of us one of the most exciting paths given to human beings in their eternally challenging excitement of being alive. All we have to do is take it.

II

To convey the story of the Prodigal Son in dance would be one of the greatest challenges a contemporary choreographer could meet. But such a dance would have to be as short, simple, and sweet as the original telling in Luke.

It is a great question in my mind whether we have in our theatre dance found the vocabulary to tell such a story with the required

45

directness and simplicity. The movement language used for such a dance would have to be consonant with the way the story was originally told to succeed as a worthy work of art. The first requirement for the use of such a story in dance would be the sincerity of the choreographer in his desire to tell the story, and tell only the story and nothing but the story.

There are two errors that I believe would be immediate temptations: one, allowing a movement to be used that did not absolutely, directly contribute to the immediacy of the telling; second, using the lines "devoured thy living with harlots" and "wasted his substance with riotous living" as an excuse completely out of proportion to the main telling of the parable for a scene of titillation and display of sex for sex-starved Americans.

Unless the spiritual meaning of the parable was uppermost in the mind of the choreographer at every stage and moment of the work, he should not attempt it. He had better wait until he is inwardly ready.

Dr. F. S. C. Northrop of Yale, author of *The Meeting of East and West,* formulates the most important aesthetic distinction in the history of Western thought when he uses the term "art in its first function" for the art that is concerned only with the materials of art in and for their own sake, because of their ineffable capacity to pinpoint the wondrous, living moment. This is not to be confused with "art for art's sake." The meaning of "art in its first function" can be distinguished by defining "art in its second function" as the art that uses the materials — the colors, shapes, sounds, and movements — not just for their own sake but to convey by means of them something in human experience other than the mysterious, sensuous aliveness of these colors, shapes, sounds, and movements.

When the choreographer presents movement in and for its own sake, he is not communicating. He is then not using the movement as a language. He is not "saying" something. The movement just "is." This difficult innocence of the pure fact of movement just "being" in and for itself, before it communicates, yields that strange, holy center that is the only thing we know about being alive. Such

47

movement has its own significant purpose of filling the audience with wonder and delight, and that is very special and very perfect and more valuable than anything in the world. But it is not communication. It is before and beyond communication. It simply is!

When the choreographer sets out to do more — to use the movements not for their own sake but for the sake of revealing some theme, some idea, some narrative — then he must make the movement into a language. He must communicate with this language. One can sum it up this way:

> When uncommunicating, be wondrous.
> When communicating, communicate.

To invent movement to keep pointing directly at the story of the Prodigal Son at the present stage of dance, without falling into mime, would be extremely difficult, if what one sees on the stage is to be powerful and equivalent in intensity to the Biblical telling. There is a double requirement in this case. Each movement invented for the story must be as beautiful and fresh as a movement done for its own sake, but it has a second necessity. It must serve the purpose and immediacy of the story and only that.

The charm and power of the parable, and of course the truth, would be the first concern. Certainly it charms us, for it is a beautiful *peripeteia* (reversal); though in the opposite sense to downfall, as in Greek tragedy. Here it is not catastrophe, but a return and upcoming, or rebirth, the courage of the hero to grow up. The story is poignant and, like all true tragedies, the ending shows new sight, growth, and especially joy. When we see the hero come to self-knowledge, we are full of joy, because we see there is the chance that we ourselves can come to self-knowledge and so to our maturity. When the theatre does this, each man and woman walks out renewed.

This is the most exciting and profound aim of art in its second function — to embody and convey to the audience the artist's deepest insights — and not just his own, but those of the wisest thinkers of his or any time. For the artist, most completely when he is using art in its second function, is a priest and not just a reporter.

48

Rather than be concerned with any personalized treatment of the parable, my goal would be to present it stark and naked.

The cast would have: the Father, the Younger Son who leaves home, the Older Son who stays, the Citizen of the Far Country, three Women of the Father's House. I would use the Citizen very briefly as an antagonist to register the Younger Son's disintegration and degradation. I would avoid using the harlots. I would convey the Younger Son's journey, his dissipation, and his degradation through a solo passage. The conclusion of it would be his confronting the Citizen of a Far Country to highlight his final humiliation.

The most beautiful addition of thought beyond the words of the parable could be the conclusion. It would be that the Son who stayed home joined too in the making merry with a glad heart and all jealousy vanished.

For the Father appears to have made a mistake. He appears never to have told the Older Son how much he loved him. And the Older Son always needs to be told that. Most of the time we are the Older Son. And the Father, way back in Near Eastern, ancient society, behaved much like an English father. In the story, the Older Son quite humanly begs for evidence of being loved too. So his acceptance of the Father's speech that this was so, even though it had not appeared so, would be the triumph. The registering of this acceptance by the Older Son's participating in the rejoicing would be to show the greatest maturity and completeness. The greatest triumph!

I would use no setting in the sense of painted backdrop or any other device that would make the place of the stage too fixed. I might delimit sections of the stage to show the Father's house at the beginning and end, and other sections for the journey, and maybe there would be a fairly delimited part in which all the action in the Far Country would be contained.

The beauty of the objects that the dancers use would visually enhance the action and clarify the narrative. So I see used the robe, the ring, the shoes, but not the fatted calf. Stage objects are worse than useless, however, if they are used only to convey meaning. I am satisfied only by the approach of artists like Isamu Noguchi and

Ralph Dorazio, who have known the principle that everything used on the stage must be beautiful in its own materials, in its own right. To me, the only meaningful theatre aesthetic would be one in which every object used on stage and the making of every costume must be as beautiful in its construction and material on the side never seen by the audience as on the side that is seen.

I would compose the dance first, complete to the last rhythmic subdivision of a pulse, as I have done in all choreography since 1951. Then I would commission the musical score. Especially for works with a plot line, this allows the choreographer to hew to the line of meaning, pulse by pulse. It avoids padding, because music written after the dance is finished can be composed to fit the dramatic or movement requirements exactly. Even a score written to a scenario cannot achieve this exactness. Likewise, it allows the choreographer to extend his action to complete his meaning. It keeps the musician from digressing into musical ends that may distract from the intent of the dance, or at least make that intent diffuse. Such a method is feasible only if a brilliant composer and theatre person like Lucia Dlugoszewski is willing to compose the score to the completed dance and yet make an equal work of art, not a subservient one. I would suggest that Miss Dlugoszewski score the work for five or six instruments. In general, too much "weight" of sound buries the appropriate kinesthetic experience in the dancer. The finest theatre and dance music all over the known world uses only a few instruments at a time to accompany dance — except in the greedy West.

I think it is almost impossible to speak of aspects of the movement, such as its style, before it is found, before it comes out of my body as I choreograph, as a spider spins its web out of its body. My goal, however, in terms of quality, would be to make it economical. I would like it to be as economical as Brancusi's Fish or Seal or Flying Turtle. The meaning is conveyed, and this is defined, clear, and beautiful. But the means to convey this meaning in themselves require meeting the greater challenge — that the means, the materials of the art, are defined and clear and beautiful and imaginative and inventive.

Because of the crumbling of a generally experienced ground of metaphysics, or myth, or doctrine, the artist in modern times has fallen into the trap of thinking that he is wise enough to originate ideas. What has developed is a notion that the artist's job is to express what Coomaraswamy calls the artist's "private emotional storms." In this day of commercialism and competition, the artist has allowed himself to capitalize on eccentricity and dreaming up personal styles, gimmicks, and expression. Coomaraswamy contrasts this with the traditional role of the artist in societies where art has been used as a total expression of everyone's common life, either before the Renaissance or in any non-Western society. There art has been used to lead the spectator to "liberation" — to self-knowledge, or truth. We in a transcending society have the added burden of restating and rediscovering these original intuitions, as science in its own way continually puts them on trial. Thus the idea of using the Prodigal Son as a dance serves the highest purpose of art. It could eternally remind an audience of a truth without weariness, as Indian dancers have for hundreds of years danced about Krishna and his beloved. For the parable of the Prodigal Son is based on the eternal truth that "the door is always open."

Erick Hawkins
PURE POETRY

51

Donald McKayle

THE ACT OF THEATRE

I

DANCE is my medium and theatre is my home. It is here that I find
excitement and fulfillment. Anything so close and so immediate
must bear the personal stamp of the creator if it is to reach out to
the viewer in its ultimate role, which is communication. This is the
key factor: the communication between artist and audience. This is
what creates that indefinable electricity, which is essential to theatre.
Theatre is not architecture or tradition or effects — it is an act. It is
done in concert and demands collaboration all along the way from
the conception to the final moment of unveiling.

Good work may be found in all forms of dancing, for in reality
there are only two kinds — that which is well done and that which
is not. And while the finest dance can be found in the so-called concert field and the most banal in the commercial field, the words "concert" and "commercial" are not synonymous with "good" and "bad."
Some of the dances done in the commercial theatre far surpass many
of the things seen on the concert stage; some of the latter should never
have been presented at all. I believe that people come to the theatre
to be moved or entertained. They do not come to be lectured, per-
plexed by perversity, or bored by tedious obscurities, no matter how
sincerely felt. The final act of theatre is that sharing with the audience
— the collaboration that I call participation. If this can be accomplished only with a small coterie of well-versed followers, the chances
are that the artist has failed.

My thoughts are dedicated to those artists who are in the creative act of theatre, rather than to those who are engaged in preserv-

53

ing and perfecting tradition. The creators include artists in many forms — modern, ballet, and the so-called ethnic idioms. The dance theatre of today has many fine practitioners of divergent schools or points of view — but each with that personal stamp which makes for greatness. Martha Graham, Alwin Nikolais, Jerome Robbins are a few. All these people are modern (if one must find a cubbyhole to put artists into), not because they share technical devices, but because their outlook is contemporary.

The need to categorize I consider a point of contention. To me, one's alliance is determined by the manner of one's work. Is it the act of creation, or preservation? Is its aim realization or anticipation? If one must make niches, let them be based on artistic value. Classification according to arbitrary, ethnic groups is ridiculous and misleading. Some critics have discussed the work of most dance artists along the lines of their basic artistic allegiances, and then — quite separately — they have discussed the Negro dance. Yet certainly such dancers as Carmen de Lavallade and Janet Collins have much in common with Melissa Hayden and Pauline Koner. Opposition to casting dancers according to ability, talent, and dance quality rather than coloring has been defended with the argument of theatrical verisimilitude — that is, if the artist concerned is a Negro. No question is raised of José Limón's essaying the role of the Moor Othello, or of Helen Tamiris's dancing Negro spirituals, or of Hadassah's excursions into the Hindu dance. Prevailing prejudices have led any number of fine Negro ballet dancers such as Billie Wilson, Sylvester Campbell, Ronnie Aul, and Ronald Frazier to seek positions in Europe. There they have been quickly employed in ballet companies, where there are no extra-dance barriers to obscure the vision of their real abilities — such as the most recent nonsense concerning the Negro physique or that fallacious old bromide about Negro rhythm.

One's cultural heritage serves to flavor one's work, and the groups that are segregated socially, politically, and economically from the body of society tend to keep their cultural identity strongly intact, most often giving the national culture its mark of uniqueness

— witness the music, dance, and crafts of the Yemenite Jew in Israel; the song and dance of the gypsy in Spain; the tremendous contribution of the Negro to American music. One cannot help but be moved by these forces, no matter what one's birthright, and they become national and international treasures, for art knows no boundaries. They become the property of mankind, and the ability to perform within them is limited only by personal, artistic temperament and inner comprehension. This is especially true of music and dance, which have no language barriers. One cannot deny the rightness of Maria Alba dancing the *soleares* because she was not born a Spanish gypsy, or of Gerry Mulligan playing jazz because he was not born an American Negro, or of Raven Wilkinson dancing classical ballet because she is an American Negro.

If an artist is to bring anything of value to his work, he must seek his inspiration outside of the narrow confines of the technique of his craft. This is as true in dance as in the other art forms. But there is an exception. There are those artists who are dedicated to delving solely into explorations of body textures, tensions, and juxtapositions. Yes, they are valuable, and some of them will be known to posterity much like the ballet greats who first rose *sur les pointes* and added the double revolution of the pirouette. Pure movement in dance has its own validity when its practitioners are able to make their audiences respond with the very fibre of their own musculatures. There is little as exciting as a fine, virile, masculine dancer, demonstrating the completeness of physical prowess; or as thrilling as a female dancer, perfectly attuned rhythmically, muscularly, and temperamentally. Some of the finest choreography celebrates these qualities. Specific characterization is not necessary for dance to be communicative on a human level.

In my own work, I always demand a certain vibrancy, an inner vitality that communicates through the viscera, not the mind. While the mind is never dormant, it does not hold sway in all areas, and definitely should not in dance. The senses must be reached before the mind. The reflection afterward, which is then basically a process of the mind, should — if the experience has been meaningful — once

Games: choreography, Donald McKayle (photo: Jack Mitchell)

more awaken this sensory network. This is what I aim for in my dances, whether they have definite plots or are more abstract in concept.

It was a childhood memory that triggered my first dance. . . . It was dusk, and the block was dimly lit by a street lamp around which we hovered choosing a game. The street, playground of tenement children, was soon ringing with calls and cries, the happy shouts of the young. The street lamp threw a shadow large and looming — the constant spectre of fear — "Chickee the Cop!" The cry was broken; the game became a sordid dance of terror.

Games opens with songs and dances of play. Imagination that seeps out in verse converts empty beer cans into the most wonderful toys in the world. But there was also the dance of hunger. How many times we sang:

>Old Aunt Dinah sick in the bed
>Called for the doctor, the doctor said,
>All you need's some short'ning bread.

And then to terror — the terror of old, of the plantation overseer . . .

>There is your master; there is your mister
>There is the one gonna bring you to blister.

To today . . .

>Chickee the Cop!
>I saw a cop a walkin' down the street
>Swingin' his billie and a struttin' his beat.
>He's gonna catch you, beat you hard,
>Bash all of your bones, so help me God.

From remembrance came a dance.

Nocturne is a lyric dance that grew out of a first love with the music of Moondog. Its basic material is pure movement, yet it is not movement in a void of mood or idea. The dance celebrates the qualities of man and woman. Man is depicted in his role of discoverer, protector; woman as inspirer. The male patterns are large, thrusting, laced with impulse, volatility, and expectation. The female movements are flowing, curved, inviting. The resulting duets are a blending of both qualities.

57

District Storyville: choreography, Donald McKayle: Carmen de Lavallade and ensemble (photo: Herbert Migdoll)

Then I became intrigued with the music of the Southern Negro chain gang. What first captured me were the pulsing, restless rhythms. They seemed wrapped in the chains that bound the suffering men together, and they seemed to explode in desperation and anger. The lyrics were sardonic and then, in turn, biting, sensual, and filled with protest. The incessant labor of the men is the background for the drama. Their dreams, as envisioned in their desire for freedom, come always in the guise of a woman — once as the essence of idealized femininity; then as the remembered figures of sweetheart, mother, and wife. In retrospect, I find in *Rainbow Round My Shoulder* the same theme that appeared in *Nocturne* — woman, the inspirer.

District Storyville and *Reflections in the Park* are both set in the jazz idiom. One is a period piece set in the notorious red-light district of New Orleans; the other is a contemporary statement of love, dreams, cruelties, and fantasies in the heart of a big city. The former draws its ideas from the beginnings of jazz, a kaleidoscope of ribaldry, decadence, and creation. In the latter, the scene is New York in its one bucolic spot — the park. Here the inhabitants of the city come to find that contrast necessary to their urban lives — but they cannot escape the encroachment of pavements, mortar, and brick. Both works have in common the urgency of the underlying jazz rhythms.

II

The scene is a ballroom in a West Indian community within an American city. The music comes from a small combination of piano, guitar, conga drum, various islands gourds, and saxophone. The combo is situated in a niche upstage, partly veiled by a series of draped gauzes, which also permit various upstage entrances. Two projected downstage balconies mark a horseshoe mezzanine arrangement. A globe dominates the overhead. Two small tables and chairs are situated upstage right and left, and glimpses of others can be seen within the wings. The flow of bias chiffon dresses, bertha collars, and the highlights of marcelled coiffures place the era in the 1930's, as do the piano player's riffs and the lilt of the movement. The mood of joviality is set in an opening dance. We are made aware of a close community feeling, and are introduced to the leading club members: an extravagant dowager, her rather quietly dignified mate, and their young daughter — the main debutante of the evening. At the end of this dance, the major characters enter: a family consisting of a young man, his father, and his mother. In the next dance, the young girl and boy are presented to each other to the strains of a West Indian waltz. The circling globe colors the moving figures, and within the changing and interweaving couples, we are made aware of filial responsibilities and parental approval and the budding of first awareness.

The following episode is a dynamic dance done as an entertainment by a dancer. Her partner is her paramour, and his role is to perform primarily as a musician, playing sticks on a long conga drum, which he straddles. The band backs up the dance, all the instruments being used in the manner of a percussion ensemble. The young boy, who is downstage left, is in a direct line of vision to the drummer, who is downstage right. Between them is the dancer. The attraction of the boy to the dancer is apparent to her. At the crescendo of the dance, she runs from the corner where the young boy is standing, leaps up on the drum — which has been driving her on relentlessly — and stops the drummer's hands.

As the entertainers take their bows and leave, the boy starts in the direction of the dancer, but is swept away by the dowager into position for the grand march. The young girl is crowned and accepts the boy's hand, as the party slips into the stately measures of the Castillian. Couples begin to take their leave. As the lights are dimmed, the boy returns to claim the forgotten sceptre of the young girl. It has been found by the dancer, who goes through a small, wistful pantomime. He crowns her from behind with the debutante's diadem, which he has been carrying. She returns his gallantry with a toast. Under the strum of the solo guitar, we hear the invitation of the maracatu. The dance grows wilder. We see the boy on the threshold of manhood, happy within the confines of his parents' world as typified by his acceptance of the graciousness of the young girl. Suddenly he tastes the strange fruits of another world and becomes intoxicated with this new excitement. The dancer, experienced in her ways, is touched by the ingenuousness of her new companion. The drummer enters. He attacks the boy brutally, and takes his possessions. The dancer defends the lad. The entertainers battle, and their conflict grows into an animalistic love dance. The drummer carries her off.

The theme of the waltz presentation is stated again as the young girl and her parents return to find the boy in what is apparently a drunken stupor; the crown at his side, the sceptre in his hand. The boy awakens to find them turning on him and leaving. His father enters. The boy looks desperately around for the dancer, but finds only the unfinished wine, which he consumes. He approaches his father, slowly falling into his arms, drunk with wine and with the physical and spiritual brutality of love that has been born and slaughtered. As they exit, the dancer enters on the upper balcony. The drummer's sticks can be heard in violent rhythmic contrast to the waltz as the curtain falls.

Alwin Nikolais

I

IT is impossible for me to be a purist; my loves are too many for that. I am excited by things very old and also very new, and by so many things in between as well.

Thus, I cannot be content as only a choreographer. As such, my dominant concern should be motion; yet I cannot forego my attraction to the shapes and forms of things. Therefore, I do not hesitate to stress a sculptural form to the exclusion of motional excitement. Nor can I divorce myself from strong passions for sound and color, so I invade the fields of the composer and the painter as well. In truth, then, I am not a devoted husband to dance, for I choose to marry the lot of my inamorati rather than swearing fixed fidelity to one.

I look upon this polygamy of motion, shape, color, and sound as the basic art of the theatre. To me, the art of drama is one thing; the art of theatre is another. In the latter, a magical panorama of things, sounds, colors, shapes, lights, illusions, and events happen before your eyes and your ears. I find my needs cannot be wholly satisfied by one art. I like to mix my magics.

We are now in a new period of modern dance, and it is a period of new freedom. All the arts, we find, are now becoming vitally concerned with the direct and poignant translation of those abstract elements that characterize and underline an art subject. Not that earlier periods have ignored the inner substance. They have, however, usually spelled it out in terms of a literal scene. Freedom from the domination of the concrete is a logical manifestation of our times.

One of the most striking characteristics of the new art is the

63

Alwin Nikolais (photo: Eric Sutherland: Walker Art Center)

freedom from the literal and peripheral self of man. The artist need no longer channel his subject through a finite scene, nor need he distort, enlarge, reduce, or eliminate part of it to release its inner content. What is more, he is free of the subject-vehicle demanded by fixation and reference to the literal scene.

The early modern dance explored the psyche. Its concepts involved man's concern with the joys and pains of self-discovery. The idea was poetically translated into a kinetic language enacted by the dance character through whom a moment of psychological drama transpired. In the new art, the dance character is no longer dominant. The new dance figure is significant more in its instrumental sensitivity and capacity to speak directly in terms of motion, shape, time, and space. It is the poetry of these elements, speaking directly out of themselves and their interrelationships rather than through a dominant character. The character may be present, but if it is, it is in equilibrium with the aggregate of all the elements in operation.

I see things best in abstract terms. To me, abstraction does not eliminate emotion. Certainly the comparison between a Bach fugue and MacDowell's "In an Indian Hunting Lodge" well illustrates this point. I look upon statements that describe my work as cold, calculating, and out-of-this-world dehumanization with considerable skepticism. I feel that some of these reflect a limited view of humanity. The greatest gifts given to man are his ability to think in terms of abstraction and his ability of transcendence. From these he derives his imaginative power. These are part of his major distinction from the lower animals. Although we need our moments of hearts and flowers, we need also to see the other side of the universal fence.

Today we hear much talk about the "non-verbal" aspects of communication. In the main, this refers to man's facility to sense meaning beyond the literal and materialistic surface. Now we can find meaning in this way, both with the hearts-and-flowers subject and with the dadaistic relation to a cigar-store Indian and a strip-teaser. Each can be an aesthetic triumph or a dud. The form of the communication is less important than the aesthetic semantics of the event itself. (In a recent review of a dance-theatre recital, I was appalled to find that the critic had singled out the piece that was the weakest aesthetically as the only worthy one of the evening. This judgment seemed to be made on the basis that this piece was more recognizable as dance. What a miserable criterion for art dance!) In any case, I feel that the so-called dehumanization can be equally, vitally communicative, and that time and the artist must decide the form.

I have particular points of view about the difference between the male and female mind in respect to abstraction, but I had better not get involved with that here. What I'd like to point out is that the male is far more inclined toward the abstract, and the field of dance is overpoweringly female and matriarchal. I hope fervently for the time when the socio-dynamic climate will re-establish the male in a more just position in the modern dance world.

The choreographer of the new period of the modern dance is concerned with basic and legitimate elements, and is imbued with the urgency of pursuing the fleeting banshee of the moment of art according to the dictates of his individual vision.

II

I was once asked to create the choreography for a proposed Broadway musical production of an adaptation of Aldous Huxley's *Brave New World*. After several conferences with the producer, writer, and sundry other people associated with the project, I asked myself if — left on my own — I would ever want to choreograph a "feelie." I concluded that I would not.

Now, faced with the hypothetical project of creating a dance-theatre piece based on *The Prodigal Son,* the same question arises. This particular subject excites me even less than the Huxley. The bribe of hypothetical, unlimited funds seems not to affect my view; although I can think of one kind of production that would require Canaveral-like financial launching (but this I'll go into later). For me, *Brave New World* would offer far greater aesthetic challenge then *The Prodigal Son,* and would do justice to a plump budget. Even so, I prefer to avoid it.

There are times when an artist must turn his creative machineries to an idea offered by someone else. I have done this many times. Usually, one does this either because of economic need or because the opportunity offers advantages to personal development. But for me — unless it were a very special commission, one well suited to me — I would consider such a situation only a distraction from what I really want to do. Assuming, however, that this circumstance was challenging, and the dancers had the prospect of a good salary, I might even enjoy working with someone else's idea.

I understand that this hypothetical project is only a device to reveal the process of a particular creator's mind. I'll go along with it, but my heart is not really involved.

The Prodigal Son is a literal and relatively simple parable. Because my mind works in the direction of the non-literal or abstract, the mountain will have to come to Mohammed. Of course, this has happened many times before in dance. In ballet, particularly, a simple, literal story line has often been the tomato on which a rose is grafted. Here the story offers a skeletal framework upon which the non-literal dances are hung. In any case, I prefer to eliminate the story line and almost all literal reference, to just concentrate on the dances and theatre elements, which I am inclined to integrate into a theatre (happening). (By this I do not mean theatre as drama, but theatre as a form of musicality, of motion, light, color, sound, etc.)

So you can see this whole project is out of the range of my present congenialities. Nevertheless, I'll go on.

The Prodigal Son is a simple parable, but it can be seen from many points of view. The restless son leaves home to spend his inheritance willy-nilly and sow his wild oats, while his brothers invest their cash and lives in homebody stock. The son returns home broke, and is given a loving, extravagant welcome by the parents — much to the outrage of the brothers.

The interpretations the parable offers are numerous. It could be comedy or tragedy. It could be looked upon politically, as a lesson in finance, philosophically, psychologically, or as any combination of these.

The reason the son leaves home is not wholly apparent in the Bible. So to establish his behavior pattern in dance, we would have to give him some background to explain his act. He could be a fool or a hero; lovable or obnoxious; a brilliant, witty, satirical character; or a dolt. We could endow him with the vitality and bravado of a restless, inquisitive spirit. We could generously endow him with a passion for exploration and the courage to rub shoulders expansively with the universe, paired with a willingness to take his consequences and measurement therefrom. The Bible implies that he is somewhat rash and unwise in his fling. Yet we could take some artistic liberty here by motivating his behavior. The more one analyzes, the more it is evident that the theme offers much to a writer — perhaps more than to a choreographer. As a matter of fact, we have elements here of the Oedipus story, *The Silver Cord, Waiting for Godot, You Can't Go Home Again*, and many others.

With a little deep thinking, we could go almost anywhere. The son could represent the healthy soul who defies tradition, conformity, adherence to the status quo, and all else that supposedly stagnates the evolution of human capacity. On the other hand, he could be villain of the piece; insensitive to the consequences of his acts, unrealistic about his responsibilities as a member of the family, and welcomed back only because of some peculiar psycho-biological factor indigenous to human parenthood.

The abstractionist cannot be excused from this analytical investigation. As a matter of fact, for him it is even more essential, for — as the superficial, literal physicalities are removed — the molecular substance beneath must then do the speaking.

Even as I write this, I must confess that the intellectualizing process above is not my way of doing. I prefer to drop a simple, single idea into my brain and let it rummage around for several months, with no particular efforts toward consciousness on my part. Then, two or three weeks before I begin to choreograph, I attempt to cast up the results of the Rorschach process. Then I like to choreograph swiftly and within a short span of time. I feel that in this outpouring I keep the channels of my subject open. Even here, I do not over-

Imago: choreography, Alwin Nikolais (photo: Robert Sosenko)

question it. I like very much what one fine critic wrote of my theatre piece *Imago*. It reflects somewhat on the process I have just described:

"*Imago* is mindful of the film *Ballet Méchanique* of 30 years ago . . . also suggests the playwrights Capek, *R.U.R.,* or even *The Life of Insects*. Passed through the alembic of the choreographer's own personality and studded with the astonishing stratagems and devices of his mind and eye, they come out new all over again in *Imago*. The chief impact is not the cozy comfort of meeting old friends, but its subtly disturbing feeling. It is an atavastic uneasiness dating to the paleo-times when unknown things haunted men. There is an undeniable bit of gooseflesh in *Imago*."

This writing reflects a vision and reception far beyond the usual dehumanized-man-from-Mars stuff I am often confronted with, and I am most grateful for it.

But to get down to brass tacks. In *The Prodigal Son* we are offered four basic narrative concerns: 1, the son leaves; 2, the brothers toil; 3, the son cavorts in the world; 4, the son returns. Let us stay with Scene One.

As you may suspect, I'm not about to choreograph the brothers performing brilliant but surly grands jetés and twirls; while the mother bourrées in sadness, supported in a lamenting pas de deux by the father; while the son moons about, itching to vault over the gate.

Neither would I go in for a sort of "togetherness" idea, with a rollicking, folksy dance of the brothers, with the son not quite in the togetherness spirit and perhaps a bit show-offy on his own. In such a scene, the mother and father would perhaps offer some folksy stamps with a few humorous limps thrown in to indicate that they're not quite what they used to be. Then there would be the moment of the son's departure. Here a little Method acting, slapped onto a slow, simple three-four choreography, could add realistic heart-rending depth to the scene. (As you may perhaps note, I am impatient with the implication that dancers should be actors and tell stories. Of course they can be, and we know of many such beautiful ballets and

theatre pieces, but I don't like at all any implication that the substance of dance rests wholly in this area. It does not.)

One could attack Scene One by slanting it toward the psychological implications. A relatively few years ago, it would have been expected to have the symbolism of the umbilical cord. Such a scene would likely start with the mother doing a sort of rocking dance, while knitting a thing from an endless, thick strand of cord. The finished end of the knitting could trail offstage. There it is pulled and caused to unravel as fast as the mother knits. It is the son who does the pulling, and in this act he is drawn onstage, revealing himself as the culprit. Then the brothers come in, getting enmeshed in the cord; whereupon there could be a sort of cat's cradle or even a maypole dance. The son continues to be engaged more in unraveling than constructing. The whole thing comes to a climax in a tug-of-war dance with the same cord. Obviously, it eventually breaks, catapulting the son out of the family orbit.

In all this, the father could be busily engaged with some sort of phallic symbolism, if he cannot manage being the symbol himself.

Some would think that, because of the cord-prop involvement, this would be my cup of tea. It isn't! Even if they put the scene on Mars.

There is another way I would not do *The Prodigal Son,* even though it approaches the abstract-expressionist point of view. The son would be in a bulk of bright yellow material against a panel of lavender. The mother would be in a huge, amorphous swath of purple; the father on stilts in an elongated blue. The brothers are bound together in a single large sack of rust-colored stuff, with their heads almost buried in it. Their background is bright green and chartreuse with streaks of sea blue, pale blue, and fiery red. The brothers manipulate this stuff in jagged, spastic gestures. The mother undulates; the father rises and sinks. The son makes clear, clean sculptural gestures, occasionally dashing into mother's swath of lavender — and brothers' rust. There are mixtures of all these stuffs, but the yellow is always more active and precise until an actual separation happens. The motion of all this color would furnish the detail of

71

Vaudeville of the Elements: choreography, Alwin Nikolais (photo: Eric Sutherland: Walker Art Center)

sensation, imparting a generality of meaning that may hit deeply. All this could be accompanied by suitable electronic sounds, in the nature of clashing steel, reverberations, feedbacks, switch clicks, with an obbligato of finger-nail scratching on a blackboard. Train sounds, automobile exhausts, and rustling time tables would add a note of symbolic realism; while baby cryings, filtered and played backward, fast and slow — although not real — would actually get under the skin. Lighting could add its dimension by burning into the yellow, while other lights play kaleidoscopically on the remaining colors. An occasional light directed at the audience could give it an intimate "I mean you" sort of suggestion, while at the same time creating a retinal confusion that would add to the visual maelstrom.

There is the possibility of a dada, or absurd, approach to this scene. One of the major figures in this event could be a naked female with one foot in a steaming pot-au-feu and the other fitted with a bicycle wheel. On her head is a weathervane, and she holds a 1916 Baedeker in her hand. The mother keeps pouring whitewash over her son's head, and tries to towel it off while prancing violently. The father hammers large spikes into a tinker-toy construction, while the brothers play basketball with a garbage pail. Accompanying sounds could be sawing wood, a Florence Foster Jenkins rendition of "Home, Sweet Home," plus deep-sea recordings of the sounds of shrimps. Put all this together with the title *The Prodigal Son,* and it is bound to be meaningful to someone, and even several — if not all.

But there is the possibility of an extravagant version that might have some slight appeal to me. Perhaps you'd have difficulty understanding my descriptions if you haven't actually seen Bryce Canyon in Utah. This is an extravagantly beautiful canyon with literally thousands upon thousands of stalagmite shapes (caused by erosion), piercing upward from the canyon floor. The idea here would be to do *The Prodigal Son* in the form of a "lumière." This is a kind of spectacle popular in Europe, taking place usually at some historical edifice, castle, or palace. Colored light illuminates the building, changing color and location according to a broadcast script, sound effects,

73

Allegory: choreography, Alwin Nikolais (photo: David Berlin)

music, etc. Can you imagine the effectiveness of such an event at Bryce Canyon?

Here the stalagmites in their multitudinous shapes can be made to represent everything from cabbages to metropolises, or even to suggest abstractly any frame of mind. A cast of a few hundred, maneuvered in this wilderness of natural beauty, together with a vast number of lighting instruments (all controlled electronically), with sound score and occasional narration — this could make possible the production of almost anything from *Ben Hur* to *Fanny Hill*. It might even work out financially, with the State of Utah contributing generously because of its tourist-attraction potential. Anyway . . . there it is.

Although I have presented all the above possibilities in a somewhat snide way, I would like to say that I sincerely believe someone could manage any one of them with legitimate and elegant aesthetic results.

Whichever way it might be done, and aesthetically successful or no; some would like it . . . some would hate it . . . some would say it is dance . . . some would say not. Some would lament the lack of progress it offers to dance . . . some would lament that it does not have the old-fashioned values.

An art is not responsible for its own reception and quality. The responsibility rests with the state of culture out of which it arises. It is not a separate entity grafted upon a people. It arises from the qualities that characterize the society from which it stems. If the society is a crazy, mixed-up mess, then it is likely that the art will illuminate that fact. If it is tight and moralistic, the art will reflect that. As a matter of fact, this is part of the function of art. It defines the culture of a people. By itself, art cannot change its heritage.

So, as you perhaps guess, I have no intention of saying how I would do *The Prodigal Son*. Aside from my personal attitude toward it, I would have company difficulties. Murray Louis would play the son, and he would do well in any of the versions. Phyllis Lamhut or Gladys Bailin would get stuck with the role of the mother and would certainly hate it. (Phyllis would rather do the lady with the Bae-

74

deker.) Unless we could integrate the family, my Negro dancers, Bill Frank and Raymond Johnson, would be without roles.

In closing, I should probably reveal that I myself am a Prodigal Son. Except I haven't as yet spent my fortune, and — at the moment — I have no intention of returning home.

Pauline Koner

I

MODERN dance — I would rather think of it as intrinsic dance — basic, essential, organic, internal — as opposed to extrinsic, the kind of dance that is composed from the outside, not motivated by the inner necessity of the creator's being. I find so much in dance today that seems to come only from concern for peripheral movement and external design, rather than from the organic, emotional need. I don't feel there is the need to say something. There is the desire to say it, a rationalization, which is quite different. The inner urgency is lacking.

Most of what is done now goes about as deep as the epidermis; it is all designed from the skin out. Design is important, but what is more important is what goes from the skin in, right to the core — the center of our being. The early modern dance dug way in. One was often unaware of its external design because one was so concerned with its inner meaning. It filtered through the pores as well as through the visual line. There was something in it like the *cante jondo* (deep song) of Spanish flamenco, which is a seeking within, going into yourself to find the depth and stay with the source.

Dancers are asked, more and more, to be just bodies for the choreographer. And the choreographer uses these bodies for the design in space rather than for the artistic need to communicate. If the artistic need were there, he would demand depth of performance from each individual. With increasing neglect in this realm, sad things are happening to our new crop of young dancers. I have the feeling that in this younger generation there are more "doers" and fewer "dancers." The element of the doing has become the main goal,

Pauline Koner: in rehearsal (photo: Peter Basch)

77

the criterion, while the real essence of the dancing — the artistry — is lost sight of. There are few young dancers today who leave one with the feeling: "This is the person I cannot forget; I don't care what he did, I don't remember what he did. But I cannot forget the person; I cannot forget the presence."

Today's modern dancer thinks too technically. He becomes too involved with: "How do you do it? Where does the foot go? Where is the arm?" And I say: "Don't analyze. I want a particular quality; just do the shape of the movement and you will fall into the right lines, because I have not done it from the impulse of outer design. When you analyze too much, you are apt to lose the original movement. It does not come from outer analysis, but from an inner motivation, and therefore the dynamics and the urgency should force the muscles to go so far and no farther."

Nowadays one does not feel the sense of inner urgency in the performer. The face rarely reflects what is going on in intensity. Emotional changes, when they are really there, can't be hidden. There is something that comes out of an eye even when it is slanted down — or the angle of the head — the muscle tensions change in the face. I don't see this happening. The face is plain — it is plain because it is probably counting like mad. The design is visible, and the design is perfect to the count. It is all one color, because counts do not change in dynamics. If you listen to yourself, to the throbbing blood pulse of your body, to its breathing, to the inner singing, you find an entirely different color in your movement than if you are listening to a number.

Margot Fonteyn dances with her inner ear because she is listening to how she feels, because she experiences the moment of doing as a moment of living. Therefore she phrases. When she dances with a man, you feel she relates to the man. She "is" with the other person. Usually dancing a duet is "being" with another person; dancing with a man has to have a man-woman relationship even if you are a dryad. This awareness creates characterization, timing, and luminous quality.

It seems to me that, also in life today, people relate from the skin out instead of from the inside. The emphasis is on external relationship, on being with people, hearing the noise, hearing the sounds of voices, but not understanding anything about the people the voices belong to. This cannot produce art. Compassion is the root of all art; the artist must know compassion to create real art. The great painters — El Greco, Goya, Michelangelo, Rembrandt — they are great not because of their craftsmanship (which is indeed monumental), but because of their tremendous knowledge of human beings and their feeling for humanity.

The artist has to search, to explore all the levels of human emotion and experience, to seek and know compassion earnestly, deeply. To distill this into the best possible conscious form that he is capable of and by so doing to share this experience with an audience, to illuminate and transcend a particular moment in time — this is the function of the artist. His aim is to reach men's hearts, to reveal to them that they are more than they think they are, to strip away the layers of veneer so they can look at themselves and say: "This is how I feel, this is how I think." It is the artist's duty to crack the shell and reach the kernel, giving from the inner being to the inner being. What hurts the modern dance today is the kind of superficiality that has replaced the substance — the coldness that has replaced the compassion.

I always need a reason to work. For me, it is not just turning out another dance, like a machine. Some people work this way. These I think of as "nothing" people; the ones who make a conscious effort to have no emotion, no idea, no anything. Then there are "thing" people. These get involved with gadgets and mechanisms, and the thing is more important to them than the person. Fortunately, there are also "people" people. They look and dig and ask questions and search for answers.

For me, the work of the "nothing" people has little validity. If they find the world meaningless and confusing and say just that, there is not much reason to make the statement. We don't go to the theatre to be presented with just reality as such. An artist should not only mirror his time, but reflect upon it.

The "thing" people have made some wonderful experiments, which have enlarged the potential, opened our imagination to what one can achieve in design, in space, and in sound. But if this is an end in itself, there is a point where it defeats itself. If these devices are used as a means to an end, however, and are used purposefully to make a statement or to transfer an experience beyond the experience of the design itself, then they become valid and vital.

It is easier to be a "nothing" person or a "thing" person than a "people" person. It is harder to dig, to try to fathom an experience of your own, to understand the truth of it, and to create something out of it. This is a longer process, a more difficult process — and it can be agonizing. Many people today do not want this; they want the easy way. They are afraid, so now we find ourselves in a kind of blinker period, where people think that, if they shut out an awareness of problems, the problems will cease to exist. They will not. When one does make the effort to say something — something that reaches people, that touches them, moves them — the experience is shared.

Doris Humphrey did this. She never resolved her pieces on a negative note. This was part of her greatness. No matter how desperate the material was, the resolution was positive. She always said she believed in the wonder of the human spirit. Since, for me, this is basic, I felt a complete rapport with her manner of thinking and doing. There are people to whom the negative attitude, the hopelessness, seems to be the purpose in making something. To me, in times of hopelessness, the only way to go on living is for the artist to point out some way of hope. The person who only mirrors his period is not doing what an artist should do: act as a catalyst in society. If he sees only what is, he is merely saying in other words what everyone already knows. He is not seeing beyond; he is not transcending the immediate. The artist should ask: "How does one challenge this? How does one make life meaningful?"

The artist must comment. I do not mean that he has to narrate a parable or leave a motto. But the reflex reaction to an experience is not enough; the work must have a viewpoint. There has to be a

81

Pauline Koner (photo: Peter Basch)

conscious rethinking that forces him to see objectively, to re-evaluate, and then comment is inevitable. In rethinking, reliving an experience, he puts himself in another dimension of that experience. In the creation of art, he must analyze his own experience, seeing it objectively even as he is feeling it subjectively. He tries to be at once the viewer and the viewed. When he understands his own feeling, he can create something consciously about that understanding. He must re-establish how he felt within the experience in order to perform it with complete conviction and utter truth. Then he has a double knowledge. This is vital to art, the integration of the subjective and the objective. With such understanding, one can communicate.

Dance is a marvelous medium for such communication. For we dancers ourselves, via ourselves, our own bodies, with nothing in between — no added element such as words or colors or musical instruments — we are able to transfer an experience to another. We can identify with the other, with the audience, with the receiver — and the receiver with us — in a closer way because that person has the identical instrument we have: the body. The body sends a message from a giving muscle to a receiving muscle; the spirit sends a current of emotion to a receiving emotion.

Though the primary level of communication in dance is emotional, there may be an intellectual level as well. We feel an emotional response in just being happy, but how happy and why happy involve the mind. Each person experiences his own "how" and his own "why." The artist can stimulate this in two ways. He can embody his personal attitudes in a specific narrative form. Or he can distill the essence of an emotion, letting the viewer use it as a springboard for an experience of his own. One should try to find the ultimate in the immediate.

When I choreographed *Cassandra,* I was dealing with a specific, dramatic character, but I saw her also as a symbol of woman lamenting for her nation or for the world or for the blindness of human beings. And in *The Farewell,* which was my tribute to Doris Humphrey, I thought of her immortality as what she had achieved in her lifetime and left as her legacy to young dancers. There are various understandings of immortality, and each viewer may interpret in his own way. In *Solitary Song,* however, I wanted to grasp the essence of aloneness, to provoke the viewer to feel his own kind of solitude in his own way.

The identification of performer and audience is much closer in the modern dance than it is in the classical ballet, for the modern dance uses the body in a more organic way. The ballet dancer first stood on her toes to look like an ethereal being. To use that technique for depicting human beings of today is, for me, a mistake. It always has an element of unreality, since we cannot really identify kinesthetically. In the intrinsic dance, true identification is possible. Its movements, though stylized, are not so completely removed from the movements of living, and the audience can relate to a human experience.

When formal ballet began, it was related to the thinking, the life, the manners of the court. But that living does not exist today. Ballet is still interesting, and I am not against it; I could not be, having come from that source. I feel it has a definite purpose, as decorative painting has a purpose. While we look at some kinds of dancing for the sheer display of pyrotechnics, we watch others in order to have a deep, emotional experience. Neither should eliminate the other. The complete human being needs both. We like to see a decorative ballet, and if getting up on the toes helps the decoration, makes the girl look more ethereal, and gives the body and the leg a more beautiful line, and it seems incredible to perform — that's fine. On the other hand, I don't see the need to use that technique for saying something pertinent to today. There are always exceptions to the rule, for such ballets as Antony Tudor's *Pillar of Fire* and *Lilac Garden,* Jerome Robbins' *The Cage,* and George Balanchine's *Ivesiana* evoke a deep response. But such works are rare.

The intrinsic dance should look for new movements, new styles. The realm of movement has to be broad in texture. Think of the range of colors in painting, the shades of each color, the dynamic values. In movement, I think, this has not been explored. What I see is usually done on one level of dynamics right through an entire per-

formance. One rarely sees even a change of emotion any more. The dynamic quality within the one emotion usually remains on the same level. Yet it is possible to have, for example, a gay emotion with tremendous changes of dynamic color within the realm of happiness. One can have sadness with the variations that a motivated sadness demands. For there are kinds of sadness — reminiscent, agonized, tragic. And pain. There is pain that comes from an emotional source, and there is physical pain. There are many levels of dynamics within one kind of feeling quality. This is rarely explored to the full. A dancer seems to start at one point and remain there. The subtleties, the shadings, the seeking for various kinds of intensity — the artistry, really — do not exist.

Still another element potential of dance is missing today. I rarely feel the sense of space, the vibrancy of the entire space, and the body's relation to that space — so that no matter where the body is, the whole space is alive. I see design in the arms and legs of the body. Yet the urgency to just cover space, or to make that space an integral part of the design, does not exist very much these days. This is what I call metric rather than organic movement. Air — you should touch air; handle it, breathe it, embrace it, cut through it, leap into it. It is not the "body" jumping up or running fast that is important. It is "you" leaping into the air or cutting across the stage.

Too often there are personal styles. Each dancer finds a style for himself and stays with it, repeating the language. I prefer a challenge: how can I say this in a different way for a new piece? And my methods of looking for different ways stem from Doris Humphrey, who sought movements from gesture. The result of the search, after it is worked into the dance, may be so far removed from the original source that it is hardly recognizable. But the sheer experimentation of it has yielded a different kind of movement language. When movement is derived from gesture, the design, the dynamics, and the shape of the movement take on an entirely different look.

In depicting the story of Helen Keller in *The Shining Dark,* I sought gesture themes in real sources. They are not recognizable in

85

Pauline Koner: in performance (photo: Peter Basch)

the dance, and are not supposed to be, but everything came from factual images. There was the "teaching theme"; the touching of space, the sense of an object in the hands, like the sense of the roundness of a bowl. And there was the movement of "feeling into the unknown." These gestures were so stylized and patterned that they became dance. But this choreographic approach made them different from any other kind of movements I might have created.

On the other hand, the sources of movement for *The Farewell* stem from poetic images, both those of the actual poetry used in the songs of Mahler's last movement of *Das Lied von der Erde* and from poetic and emotional images of my personal interpolation. I found inspiration for arm patterns in the ever changing shapes of tree branches, with tremor of leaves adding rhythmic color. The flowing of a brook delineated a floor design, the bubbling and gurgling was food for phrasing. The root that winds its way from a seedling to finally burst into bloom . . . images of nature spurred the imagination to seek new forms for the body. Then there is a phrase in the poem: "The leaves are falling"; and my personal reflection: "The leaves are falling, my tears are falling." The nature image and the gestures of weeping and pain offered sources for a phrase linked by the idea of "falling, dropping" — hands, isolated at the wrists, fall first high in air, then at the eyes, and finally at the viscera. This approach creates movement that is specific to the idea and an organic part of the whole. The possibilities are limited only by the measure of one's need to search and one's own imagination.

What I am seeking now is a language that is not personal to me, but that speaks the quintessence of a mood or feeling in terms that are universally recognizable. I see the possibility of this in other art forms. There are the works of the lithographer Kaethe Kollwitz, which have a tremendous sense of pathos and compassion for the human being. It is conveyed in the feeling of the body line. You cry when you look at these; the drawings themselves cry. Strangely enough, I found that the line of the back and the head that she had in all her drawings is exactly what I use in *Solitary Song,* though I was not conscious of this when I was working on it. I am making collections of such things now. They give me courage, for otherwise one can always feel that one is just manufacturing these things, which is wrong. I feel there are certain root manifestations that are indigenous to particular emotions, and all intrinsic artists draw upon them. It is through these elemental symbols that an experience is shared by artist and audience.

II

Music: LUKAS FOSS

Set: PETER LARKIN

Narration: ARCHIBALD MACLEISH

The settings and costumes should have a timeless quality. The entire mood should maintain a symbolic reference. The scenes are not connected in narrative form, but are flashes of isolated episodes.

Scene I. The Home.

A mother, father, and two sons perform a dance that has ritual overtones. The faces of the family are covered with a gauze, which opaques the features but is transparent from within. All but the youngest son carry masks on sticks with which they cover their faces as though at a masked ball. (The masks are identical.) The youngest son is presented with a mask which he is constantly inverting so that its face is down and his own face is revealed. When a gauze is about to be placed on his face as a sort of initiation rite, the young son, refusing to conform, ceremoniously hangs up his mask and exits. Blackout.

Scene II. Somewhere — anywhere.

The background is a huge computing machine — three-dimensional — upstage center on a level or suspended. Extended from the machine are poles from which hang strings like those used for marionettes. The machine is brilliantly lit. Ten dancers in deep colors are attached to the marionette strings. One harness is empty.

87

The narration is written as a monologue for the machine over a background of sparse sounds punctuated with silences. The machine thinks aloud, announces its findings about manners, mores, and emotions. The people respond accordingly in duets, trios, or ensembles. One of the announcements is about ideal mates, which motivates a duet that is mechanical, ironic, and macabre. The various dances run a gamut of emotional colors and ideas, always resolving with a leitmotif done in unison.

The Prodigal enters and tries to relate to various people. He does a duet with a boy, who suddenly is not taking inspiration from the machine but is following the Prodigal's movement. The Prodigal cuts the strings of this boy, who then goes berserk and finally falls limp. The Prodigal puts him back in the empty harness, and he functions again quite happily. The Prodigal exits. Blackout.

Scene III. Somewhere in a City.
A group of dancers, with faces blocked out by gauze, wear masks on the backs of their heads, all of which look individual. The Prodigal has a series of encounters. At the end of each, he is surrounded, swallowed up, or overwhelmed by a mass of uniform gauze faces. Each group wants to absorb him or crush him. Each group would have a particular characteristic — one of play, one of drinking, etc. The people in the background would maintain a monotonous ground base, which would stop and start in counterpoint to the actions of the focal group. Some of these sequences would be in silence, or to electronic sound or to voice, etc. From time to time, a girl, pinspotted, wanders through aimlessly, always at a distance, and disappears. The group slowly drifts offstage, leaving the girl alone. Only the Prodigal is onstage with her. They draw together and do a warm, touching duet. In finding her, he seems to find himself. But at the end of the dance, in a final embrace, he brushes her long hair forward to reveal a simpering mask on the back of her head. Simultaneously, heads with similar masks thrust in at him from the wings and from various levels of the stage. They begin to converge on him. He flees. Blackout.

Scene IV. Same as Scene I. *The Home.*

The Prodigal enters. The formal dance, the ritual, begins again. But this time the faces of the family are not covered with gauze. The real faces are there, the stick masks covering and then revealing the reality. The Prodigal takes up his own mask, and all do a dance of formal celebration, where the masks are used as an implement of design, while the people relate to each other as individuals. The Prodigal has returned.

Pauline Koner
INTRINSIC DANCE

Paul Taylor

DOWN WITH CHOREOGRAPHY

I

A lot of dance writers, it seems, neglect to write about what most people notice first when they go to see dancing. The writers go on about dance theories, dance history, the costumes, the music, the choreography, and even the audience. In short, everything but the thing that all dancing depends on first and last. It is time more should be said about the dancer.

Because I am closest to the members of my own company and find it easy to get enthusiastic about them, I would like to say a few things about Bettie de Jong, Elizabeth Walton, Dan Wagoner, Sharon Kinney, Danny Williams, Molly Moore, Karen Brooke, and Carolyn Adams. I do not intend to give a detailed exposé on these fine people, though that could be an interesting possibility. I just want to mention one or two things that you cannot help noticing when you work with them.

More often than not, the kind of dance we work on together turns out to be dependent on these different dancers as individuals. Sometimes their limitations are as interesting as their strong points. The finest choreography in the world does not mean a thing if the dancers are not suited to it and they look terrible. That figures.

A dancer is involved in learning to execute a dance movement precisely in shape and time. A dancer is occupied with placement, stage spacing, the quality of a leap, the softness of a foot — whether a movement goes out to the audience or spirals inward upon itself. These are some of the things a dancer is concerned with, but actually what we see is more than a foot or a curved back. We see an

91

individual, and we see what that individual is. All this exact training and dance stylization cannot abstract a body into a nonentity. A person is going to be revealed. Vanity, generosity, insecurity, warmth are some traits that have a way of coming into view. This is especially true of the kind of dance that, instead of representing specific characters, features dancing itself.

Because the body does not lie, people remark on the friendliness of Elizabeth Walton's dancing. She IS friendly. Her warmth, the way she goes out to people, spills over into the way she dances. Her body does not lie. With a little prompting she can reveal qualities of a different nature. For one dance, she needed only to hear about the female preying mantis to understand what a predatory nature looks and feels like. Or take, for instance, *Aureole*. Her hips speak truly. They are the hips of an innocent satyress.

These eight dancers are not exactly like tubes of paint with which to cover the canvas of space. Not exactly. They have character and personality, which they ASSERT. They have individual traits, and just when you think you know how to handle them they CHANGE. Not like canvas that stays stretched once and for all. They sometimes get fat or discouraged or both. They acquire feelings of inadequacy. They have birthdays. On the other hand, they develop surprising and unexpected resources in their range.

An admirable and fairly unique quality of Dan Wagoner is his weight. Not in poundage so much, although he is no mosquito, — but in the way his movements are weighted. It looks as if he were pressing against heavy water rather than air. The effect is quite different from the kind of dancing that gives the illusion of flitting or floating. The viewer is involved in seeing the energy that presses into the floor or lifts out of it. This is a quality of his that shows consistently, whether he is moving slowly or quickly, in the air or on all fours. You see him and are glad that gravity can be a dancer's partner.

His is not the kind of body that will twist into a pretzel or bend double and inside out. It is a typically masculine body — solid and a bit tight in the hips. There is no use trying to make him into a twisting mosquito. Who wants to see one, anyway? Solidity can be a limitation that works as an asset.

Because of the way I work, Dan Wagoner has another asset, which is his patience or understanding or whatever you call it when a dancer is willing to go through an unusually long and involved process of making a dance. When I start a dance, I rarely know how it is going to turn out. I just start and work in an impermanent, unorganized way. Then I go back to clarify a line that may have come to the surface. I have no qualms about changing music or dancers or throwing the whole thing out entirely. As you may guess, this routine can become disappointing to a dancer, who has worked hard and long on something that later gets erased. Especially if he feels comfortable in it. Dan is usually magnanimous in these matters. He is remarkably fast to learn anything new, which is fortunate because he may go through twenty or thirty different arrangements before we arrive at the performance one. Part of his quickness to memorize long sequences may be due to his analytical mind and part, perhaps, to the training he had in medical science before he became a dancer. If it looks as if he knows what he is doing on stage, it is because he does.

Anything Bettie de Jong may do, no matter how trivial, is usually accompanied by one of the other dancer's explaining to the rest: "Bettie is different; she is Dutch." Actually, she is from reed-land. She happens to be taller than the other girls, but even if she were the same height, she would look taller. In dance formations on stage, when you do not want her to look the tallest, you put her upstage of the others because being in the distance will make her appear shorter. Or you put her downstage so the audience will assume she just looks the tallest because she is the closest. No problem.

Blond and slender, she creates a sensation whether she dances at the Bellas Artes in Mexico City or in Paris. Evidently, she does not need her looks to be effective, though, as she proved in *Insects and Heroes* and in *Three Epitaphs* in which — unpardonably — she was entirely covered, face and all. Surprisingly (but then, she is Dutch), she can do comedy. It has nothing at all to do with her "sense of hu-

mor." She understands the absurd, and her body can translate it.

In spite of all these bonus qualities, she is a slow learner. My own particular dances never come naturally to her. Rehearsals become a siege of endurance for both of us. It does not matter, because her interest in dancing never lags, and she is always ready to try the most unlikely of arrangements. So, come performance time, she blossoms forth.

Fairly regularly, Bettie de Jong will speak of something she calls "organic dance." The rest of us always laugh and tease her about this phrase, but we know what she means, and it is worth mentioning. This "organic" has nothing to do with health food. She is referring to body logic or the way movements are put together so that they are joined functionally. Theoretically, almost any sequence of movements is possible to dance, but there are those that will feel better (though not necessarily easier) to a dancer because of their peculiar kind of muscle logic. An "un-organic" dance phrase would be one containing an extraneous movement, a foreign insertion, which prevents the body from following its natural muscular path. This insertion may seem an appropriate idea for what the choreographer is trying to say, but it remains only an idea if it does not fit into the physical logic of the phrase. It will stop the dancing. It will look false and it will usually feel false to the dancer. It is like those real plants at florists that have convincing plastic blossoms wired on. You sense there is something wrong, somewhere.

There are some dancers who achieve a kind of crystal clarity in their dancing. Perhaps it is because of clean line and precise timing. It is not usually a natural quality, but comes after years of exactitude and self-discipline. This crystal quality can often dazzle an audience with its beauty, but it is often coupled with a certain iciness. Though Sharon Kinney has the clarity, what makes her remarkable is that she also has warmth. She is a kind of heart-shaped crystal.

She is appealing in the way the look of a small child astonishes and touches us with its fragile innocence. But Sharon Kinney, in private life, is Mrs. John Binder, and though she may have small bones and enormous eyes and a child's lightness, these disarming

Tracer: Paul Taylor, Bettie de Jong

features only mask prodigious strength and maturity.

I have to curb a natural tendency to make bird dances for her, or at least curb calling them bird dances in front of her, because she has a curious dislike for anything feathered.

Her speedy grasp of new combinations, which rivals Dan Wagoner's, is something she came into the company with. The happiest satisfaction for the other dancers and me and for Helen Alkire, her teacher at Ohio State University, has been watching her develop from the company "baby" into the old pro she is now after four United States and five foreign tours.

Danny Williams, Molly Moore, Karen Brooke, and Carolyn Adams are the newer members of my company, and for that reason, rather than their considerable innate talents, they have been eased into dance roles as gently, under the circumstances, as possible. At first they had to learn several dances at once — dances that were not choreographed on them. This is a harder task in many ways than being in on the initial working out of a piece. They were thrown together with people whose quirks and working habits were unfamiliar to them and vice versa. It always takes a while for dancers to become used to each others' timings, dancewise and emotionally. For all new members, there is a difficult spell when they are not sure if they will be able to manage and are not sure what the others think of them. This time has its double insecurities, as the choreographer — in turn — is trying to find the best way to bring out the new dancers' best qualities and is trying to discover the points at which criticism will help or hinder. Depending on the individual dancer, it seems best sometimes not to criticize very much rather than risk destroying the dancer's belief in himself. Other dancers seem to ask for an iron hand and may even perform at their best if you get them angry enough. However, there is a point of no return between dancer and director. In the touring concert field, where holding a company together depends on things besides unemotional cash, there is a very fine balance to be attained concerning mutual respect between working cohorts. A lot depends on all parties' abilities to cope with one another in difficult situations. A quick calm-down after a flare-up is most helpful. For the record — but without going into details — let me say that these four dancers possess superbly controlled danders. We cope.

Martha Graham was once talking to a cab-driver, who said that he liked dancing fine; what he could not stand was choreography. That seems sensible. Some dances look like "choreography," because the dancers are not allowed to become their most interesting stage selves. I like to think of a dance as a vehicle, not necessarily for one star, but for everybody. You try to find aspects in individual dancers that can be exploited. That is what people are for — to be used. They like it. Merce Cunningham manages to do this by manipulating his dancers to move through space in a fairly democratic way. Not all lined up in a circle with a big cheese in the middle. Martha Graham does it by spookily knowing what kind of dramatic projection is the bailiwick of each of her dancers. This is what I call a group vehicle. Up with dancers; down with choreography.

II

How would I describe a dance that I had been commissioned to produce with unlimited funds — providing I used the theme of the Prodigal Son?

Although I like the idea, especially the part about the unlimited funds, I am not sure how I would plan it. Maybe I would not plan it at all. All the ideas I have for dances, carefully written down when I wake up at night thinking of things like that, seem awful in the morning.

I think the father and son characters would present a problem right off if one did not depend on program notes. George Balanchine once remarked on the impossibility of showing who is the mother-in-law in a dance. Fathers and sons are hard, too.

As for costumes and scenery and lights, I like to leave them to the designers. It seems a good idea, and a more productive one, to leave the designers alone. Just let them see the dance as many times as they like, answer their questions, and leave them to work it out in their own way. The trick is to select the right designer for the right

dance. If the results do not seem suitable, do not force the designer to do something he does not believe in. Just try another designer. The same for composers. This is where those unlimited funds come in handy.

As for the style of this imaginary project, to me, it would depend on what style I had been working in previously. It is not such a problem to gravitate into a style and continue to do dances in that style. It is harder to keep up a continuous change from one work to another. I like the idea of change, not entirely for variety's sake, but for the sake of the people in the concert audience, who may have to sit through a whole evening of one choreographer's work. If one dance is presented in a particular style and that is developed fully, it is not so interesting to reiterate. A painter is looked on suspiciously if he changes styles too often, but a choreographer is working in the theatre. The time element is different. I would like to change styles for each dance, but that is difficult. If you try to change style completely, often as not, it turns out a LITTLE different. That is something, anyway.

But "style" is a word that has several meanings, and perhaps I had better explain specifically what it means to me. Some styles, or areas, I have worked in and which I would probably not use for the Prodigal Son are:

The archaic flat style. The body is seen either flat front or flat sideways or both at the same time. In a way, the dancer is seen two-dimensionally, like a shadow puppet. My *Three Epitaphs* and *Tablet* are in the flat style. It is a paradox that some painters try to make two-dimensional paintings look like three, and some dance-makers try to make three-dimensional dancers look like two. I have been trying to get out of that style. It is too flat.

Another style I tried (in *Rebus* and *Junction* and the plague section of *Insects and Heroes*) could be related to action painting. I call it dance scribbling. The idea is to see action rather than shape or line. It works best for fast movement. It is very difficult to get the dancers to do it, because the movements must first be broken down into positions in order to be taught. Then the dancers have to get rid of the

Insects and Heroes: Paul Taylor Dance Company

positions and just throw themselves into the movement. If they are doing it right, the viewer says: "This is something! But what is it?" It looks anything but two-dimensional. But it can be a terrific mess.

After that scribbling style, I thought perhaps it was clean-up time, and I worked on *Tracer* and *Aureole*. Their style is more lyric and acceptable. Everybody knows what "lyric" means — long arms. It was interesting for me, because most of my dancers have short arms. Now they looked very lyric and long and lovely. So it seemed to be time to do an ugly dance.

Scudorama is less concerned with style than with a slightly vulgar look. The nasty things the dancers do are related, in my mind at least, to Dante's *Inferno,* which he wrote in the coarse vernacular, rather than his *Paradiso,* which he wrote in a loftier manner. It is a dance that includes uncouth gesture in its movement vocabulary, and its style is intentionally unstylish.

I would not like to say if my Prodigal Son project would be serious or comic. It would depend on many things. I like to work on a piece with an open mind — or call it a full palette. You leave as many possibilities open as you can, such as:

MOVEMENT. A range from complete stillness through the kind of exaggerated slow movement one sees in the hand of a clock, on through the fastest steps the body is capable of doing.

LINE. A range from the kind of body line that goes out through the limbs in a direct, long line toward the audience, through the kind of line that is distorted and connected with what is called "in-dancing."

SPACE. Used by inches or used infinitely. A dance can seem to be happening out in the wings as well as on the part of the stage the audience can see.

This full palette includes possibilities of stage design, titles, and everything else that can be part of a dance. Once the mind is open to this idea, the really helpful part is the restrictions. You decide what not to do. You eliminate. You try everything you can and then you eliminate. As in one section of *Ivesiana,* George Balanchine eliminated the idea of having the girl soloist ever touch the floor.

I might start with some kind of idea about the Prodigal Son, but I would not guarantee how it would turn out, because I would have to see what happened on the way. Start with too rigid an idea, stick to it, and there is a good chance the dance will become forced and lifeless. I would rather follow up an aspect that I came across in the actual rehearsals — something I did not think of originally. The aim is to do the most magical work you can — to permit the chain reaction of movement ideas, which spring from the original concept. The mind tends to think in a logical way, but magic is not logical. If dance is too logical, it becomes expected and predictable; then it can lose its life.

On the other hand, it might be interesting to start with the idea of making a lifeless, predictable dance and see where that takes you. There are no rules; just decisions. It is even possible, they say, to eliminate decisions if you adhere to the idea of making dances entirely by chance. Speaking of chance, it would seem that it is one of the most misunderstood of working methods. To those who make use of it, it has nothing to do with improvisation and is simply a way of broadening one's palette. Each person's working methods are his own business, and it is a mistake to evaluate a dance by the choreographer's way of arriving at it. Personally, I like what Edwin Denby said Lou Harrison said about chance: "I'd rather chance a choice than choose a chance."

To be free to choose from a full palette, no matter how unusual the results, has always been the prerogative of the modern dance. Modern dance? To me modern dance is a license to do what I feel is worth doing, without somebody saying that I can't do it because it does not fit into a category.

But back to the Prodigal Son and his father. I would start out with some wishy-washily formed idea, give it up if a better one appeared, perhaps attempt to break out of a previous style. I would try to broaden one part of the palette while allowing another part to drop off, and hope to find a compatible composer, designer, and lighter, who would add their own dimensions. I would try not to forget the individual dancers and their importance to my group vehicle.

101

One idea that I would start with and attempt to achieve, no matter how ruthlessly, is the idea that the stage should become a magic place and unbelievably beautiful in a curious new way that cannot be described, but would cause the viewer to say Yes, uh-huh, yes!

CONTRIBUTORS

CONTRIBUTORS

JOSÉ LIMÓN

"A man of dignity," said his citation for the Capezio Award in 1964, "whose years of intense struggle have culminated in his position as indisputably the foremost male dancer in the field of the American modern dance." Born in Mexico, José Limón knew many years of struggle before he became a leading dancer for Doris Humphrey and eventually had his own company, with Miss Humphrey as artistic director. With his group, he has toured Europe, South America, and the Orient under the auspices of the United States State Department. For many years Mr. Limón has headed the faculty of the Connecticut College School of Dance. He holds an honorary doctorate from Wesleyan University. In 1964 he was named artistic director of the American Dance Theatre, a company sponsored by the New York State Council on the Arts to serve as a repository for the repertory of the American modern dance.

ANNA SOKOLOW

Known as one of the most dynamic and uncompromising of the modern dance choreographers, Anna Sokolow began her career as a member of the Martha Graham company, forming her own group in 1937. She has worked in Mexico for the government's Ministry of Fine Arts, and in Israel, both with the Yemenite company Imbal and with her own ensemble of actor-dancers. In addition to choreographing for her New York company, Miss Sokolow has created dances for the Broadway theatre and for the Robert Joffrey Ballet. She has been in charge of training in movement for actors for the

Lincoln Center Repertory Theatre since its inception. In 1962 she received the Dance Magazine Award for a career "distinguished by integrity and creative boldness" and for her recent works, which "have opened the road to a penetratingly human approach to the jazz idiom."

ERICK HAWKINS

A graduate of Harvard (Greek literature and art), Erick Hawkins was a member of the American Ballet before 1938, when he joined the Martha Graham company and became its leading male dancer. Since 1957 he has had his own group, for which he creates dances in close collaboration with musician Lucia Dlugoszewski and designer Ralph Dorazio. The company has toured extensively in the United States and has appeared in Paris. The philosopher F. S. C. Northrop has described the dances of Erick Hawkins as evoking "the proud pleasure of being splendidly justified in living." The dancing of them he calls "unique butterfly poetry."

DONALD McKAYLE

In 1963 the Capezio Award cited Donald McKayle "for his translation of deeply rooted American folk materials . . . into theatre dances of interracial cast which faithfully reflect life in our land." A student of Martha Graham, he danced also in the companies of Anna Sokolow and Merce Cunningham. Since 1951 he has created works for his own company, as well as for television and the Broadway stage. His most recent contribution to the latter was *Golden Boy*.

ALWIN NIKOLAIS

The Director of the Henry Street Playhouse Dance Company not only choreographs his own theatre pieces but composes their musical (usually electronic) scores as well. In addition to showing his company on their own stage at the Playhouse, Mr. Nikolais has presented them at festivals in Montreal and Spoleto. His works have been seen on television films made in Canada, England, and Italy, and are known to a large public (tremendous for modern dance) through seven appearances on the Steve Allen Show. Mr. Nikolais has received commissions for new theatre works from the University of Illinois, the American Dance Festival, and the Montreal Arts Festival. In 1964 he held a Guggenheim Fellowship, and in 1965 he was commissioned by the Walker Art Foundation to create a new piece for the Tyrone Guthrie Theatre in Minneapolis.

PAULINE KONER

When she was thirteen, Michel Fokine said, "In her, the soul dances." Her career has ever since inspired similar phrases. At first a concert soloist, Miss Koner joined the company of José Limón in 1946, creating leading roles in many of the finest works of Limón and of Doris Humphrey. She has choreographed for her own group since 1949, and has become known also as a teacher, especially for her course in the art of performing, which she has given at Jacob's Pillow as well as at the Connecticut College School of Dance. In 1965 Pauline Koner spent six months in Japan, teaching and performing, as the recipient of a Fulbright-Hayes Lecturers' Grant. She is now on the faculty of the newly formed North Carolina School of the Arts.

PAUL TAYLOR

In 1957 Paul Taylor's New York concert received a review consisting of a blank white space, signed at the bottom with the critic's initials. In one dance Mr. Taylor just stood still from the time the curtain rose until it fell. It was, another critic later remarked, "something he had to get out of his system." Since then, both he and his dancers have moved a great deal — on stages throughout the United States and Europe. Mr. Taylor had first planned to be a painter. When he changed arts, he danced first with Merce Cunningham and then with Martha Graham. He has been the recipient of a Guggenheim Fellowship in choreography and of a number of commissions, including one from Spoleto's Festival of Two Worlds.